National Lampoon's

DOON

ELLIS WEINER

PUBLISHED BY POCKET BOOKS NEW YORK

Another *Original* publication of POCKET BOOKS

 POCKET BOOKS, a division of Simon & Schuster, Inc.
1230 Avenue of the Americas, New York, N.Y. 10020

ISBN: 0-671-54144-7

First Pocket Books printing November, 1984

10 9 8 7 6 5 4 3 2 1

POCKET and colophon are registered trademarks
of Simon & Schuster, Inc.

Printed in the U.S.A.

book one

DOON

———————————————————————

Know, sisters of the Boni Maroni, that any study of the life of Mauve'Bib demands the subtlest attention to details of place. Can you truly understand why a man is a thing, if you neglect to understand where he is that thing that he is?

Commence, then, with the fact that it is on the planet Cowboydan that Mauve'Bib spent his childhood—yet it is on Arruckus, the planet known as Doon, that he fulfilled his destiny. It is Doon that is his homeworld, Doon that is his place of triumph, Doon that is forever his principle mailing address.

Send therefore to Doon your requests for recipes and reprints—or send them not at all.

—from "The Making of the Messiah, 10,193," by the Princess Serutan

In the week before their departure to Arruckus, amid the hurly and the burly of the moving and the grooving, did an old woman come to planet Cowboydan to visit the mother-adult of the boy-child, Pall.

Her journey, via Schlepping Guild 'Ighliner, had been a difficult one. There had been turbulence in the Nether Region—the Guild navigators had found it necessary, not only to fold space, but to trim it and shove it as well. She entered Castle Agamemnides in foul humor.

She was escorted into living room Agamemnides, where waited the Lady Jazzica, wife to the boy-child's man-father, Duke Lotto Agamemnides.

"I would see the boy, Jazzica," the crone rasped.

"I'll . . . fetch him, Your Revved-Uppedness," Jazzica replied.

Jazzica curtseyed and left. As befitted her Boni

Maroni training, she made optimum use of the walk to the boy's bedroom to think about what was happening that very instant in the times of her life.

She comes to administer the Test, she thought. *He is capable, my son, and should perform admirably. Yet even the capable are capable—of failure!*

This stabbed a single question unbidden at her consciousness. *Has Pall applied to a backup school?*

Jazzica sought desperately to conceal her fear, lest her son perceive it and grow thus himself likewise afraid like her, too. She called upon her Boni Maroni training in body- and mind-control, the dual and complimentary disciplines known as yogi-bear and yogi-berra, to master her roiled emotions, reinstate the rationality of calm.

She arrived at his door, knocked, was admitted, entered.

Pall sat at his desk, a filmbook open before him. Jazzica noted his eyes, with their eyebrows and lids and accompanying nose, mouth, and ears.

He is like his father in that, she thought. The thought of Duke Lotto panged in her a tinge of guilt-reflex, which she stifled with her superior abilities.

"What is it, Mother?" Pall asked.

"There's a one I want you to meet, Pall," she said. "It is the Revved-Up Mother George Cynthia Mohairem. She has come to give you a . . . test."

"Is something wrong?" the boy probed.

"Why . . . no . . . Pall."

But the boy's own senses, honed keen by his own Boni Maroni training, were quick to detect in his mother those subtle signs of unease, traitors braying betrayal of her anxiety, audible to those, like him, with eyes to hear.

"But Mother, you fear something," he stated.

"I?" *The boy had learned well.* "Nonsense. What makes you say that?"

"You're trembling."

"I'm chilly."

"Your teeth are chattering."

"I'm doing my . . . jaw exercises."

"You're biting your fingernails."

"I'm . . . hungry, Pall."

The boy grew silent. Something was troubling his mother—something she chose to deny rather than explain. And he knew she knew he could perceive them—had she not been his teacher? Had she not made it her own goal, to educate her son in the Boni Maroni Ways and Means?

True, such training was unusual for a boy; the Boni Maroni order was, after all, principally composed of women.

Perhaps I am a woman, Pall thought.

But his heightened powers of observation were able to discern, between his legs and hidden from the casual observer by the clothing of his race, those telltale organs that confirmed his intuition that he was indeed a male-man.

"We must not keep Revved-Up Mother waiting," Jessica said, leading Pall out of his room.

This enigmatic summons was but one more odd event among the many that had occurred of late. Pall's mind

9

swam with the awareness of what his family was about to undertake: leaving Cowboydan, ancestral home of House Agamemnides for thirty generations, to relocate on Arruckus.

Arruckus. Doon. Dessert Planet.

Duke Lotto would administer the planet in fief, replacing Baron Vladimir Hardchargin and House Hardchargin at the invitation of the Pahdedbrah Emperor, Shaddap IV. It was an unexpected choice—all the Empire knew that the Hardchargins and the Agamemnides had for centuries been mortal enemies, having declared between them that formal state of vendetta known as kramden.

Other Great Houses were openly covetous of the Duke's honor. House Wax, House Pancakes, House Rising Sun, House Seven Betty Grables—all could be expected to make known their resentment at having been denied the fiefdom of Doon.

Pall understood some, but not all, of this. Yet certain it was that Arruckus would be his new home. It was a forbidding place—the Dessert Planet, so called because, its surface an almost unbroken expanse of sugar, its mountainous outcroppings and other geoconfectionological features mainly rock candy, it was a world virtually devoid of entrees.

And now his confusion was heightened by the appearance of this wizened crone to whom he was introduced in the living room. She was thin and bent, and wore a shapeless black robe. One of her eyes was a useless clouded orb, like shattered crystal. Her fingers were crooked and bony, her voice a sinister cackle, her nose a carrot.

10

Lady Jazzica introduced Pall. The Revved-Up Mother eyed him sourly.

Damn that Jazzica! she thought. *If only she had obeyed our command! We send her out for a pound of sweet butter and she comes back pregnant!*

"So this is our candidate for Kumkwat Haagendasz," the Revved-Up Mother mused. "What's your age, lad?"

"Fifteen, Ma'am."

"Pall," Jazzica reprimanded. "You should call her Revved-Uppedness—"

"Never mind," the old woman snapped. "He may call me anything he wants."

"'So long as he doesn't call me late for dinner,'" Pall completed the catechism.

The old woman's eye glinted amusement.

"He's a clever one, eh?" Abruptly she whirled and shot a piercing glance at Jazzica, hissed, "Leave us. We have things to discuss."

Jazzica looked into Pall's eyes, smiled, said, "I'll be back soon. Do your best. It's extremely important you pass this test—both to me, and to your father. And to your future, Pall. And . . . possibly . . . to the future of the . . . human race. But don't feel pressured." She gave him a look of worry mingled with anxiety, then left the room.

Pall tried to swallow in a dry throat. What could this test be?

"Pay attention, boy," the old woman said, and produced from within her robe a small cube, four inches on a side, each of its faces a different color. "Here. Take a good look," said the woman, handing it

11

to him with a smirk. "You may never see it this way again."

Visually probing the object more closely, Pall noticed that each face of the cube was divided into nine small squares. Suddenly the Revved-Up Mother snatched it from him, and worked it in her cold hands. Each row of squares was apparently mounted on a sophisticated form of internal pivot, for in a trice the uniformity of each face had been utterly destroyed. Now red squares mingled with yellow, blue with orange, green with white.

This is almost certainly a product of the mechanical culture of the planet Ix-Nay, Pall thought.

"Now, lad, fix it. Make it like it was," the old woman said.

Carefully Pall twisted the colored cubes. They rotated along both horizontal and vertical axes. He could see how rearranging the colors would require a three-step strategy . . .

With a rapid leap the woman was hard beside him, pressing something cold into the side of his neck. He started to turn to see what it was.

"Don't!" she hissed. "The slightest move and you die. I hold against your neck the device we call the abdul-jabbar—the high-handed, long-legged enemy. You've heard of it, perhaps?"

His head immobile, Pall said, "It's called the sky-hook, isn't it?"

"A-h-h-h-h-h, you've been taught well," she muttered. "Now let's hope you'll solve the cube. If you really are the Kumkwat Haagendasz, it shouldn't be

12

much trouble. But make one false move and you'll find my abdul-jabbar slam-dunked in your face!"

Pall tried to focus all his attention on the cube. It was fairly easy to make one side all of a single color. But as soon as he tried to complete another side, the first was disturbed, necessitating startover. And all the while, he felt the sting of the abdul-jabbar at his neck. What was this test for? And what was the Kumkwat Haagendasz?

Suddenly Pall discovered the basic pattern for positioning a color and retaining it after shifting others around. *Of course!* he thought. It required a sort of fourth-dimensional para-logical foresight—a mode of perception for which his Boni Maroni training in cooking and baking had been the ideal preparation.

But there was a thought nagged at him—that he possessed some talent or skill that other Boni Maronites did not . . .

His intuition was confirmed when the Revved-Up Mother, her eyes fixed on his hands' progress, whispered, "Kooll-juh-herk! Such skill and dexterity. He could be . . . ! He could be . . . !"

"Could be what, old woman?" Pall said, the cube now nearing completion. "Your Kumkwat Haagendasz? What's that?"

"'The One Whose Fruit-Like Soul Is Tempered to a Soft Consistency,'" she quoted by rote, echoing centuries of Boni Maroni teachings. "The One who will restore the Lost Recipe of . . ." She paused, tried to swallow in a dry throat, tried to speak through a closed mouth. ". . . of the dish that endures beyond space and time!"

13

"Like Velveeta?" Pall asked suddenly.

She gave a nod of begrudgement. "So you know of The Cheese That Cannot Die," she said. "You've learned much. Yet that is another thing."

The cube was now restored to its original pattern of colors. Pall handed it back to the old woman, felt her withdraw the abdul-jabbar.

"Does this mean I get Early Admissions?" he asked.

"Perhaps," she muttered. "Tell me, young boy-man —do you know what it is we teach?"

Pall shrugged. "Cooking. Menu planning. How to shop for seasonal life-forms."

The Revved-Up Mother scowled. "There is more! Much more!" Her eye sparkled with intensity. "We seek to refine Taste. We separate humans of discernment from the masses of humanity. There are two kinds of beings in this universe, boy: the select, and the mob. Have a care you make it your business to belong to the right one."

Pall said nothing, yet inwardly felt a stirring. The woman's words struck a chord deep within his innermost sense of things inside his *self*. He knew he was *special*—and that most of the others he met were not. And now this queer old witch spoke of the *select* . . .

The door to the room opened, and the Lady Jazzica entered. The Revved-Up Mother sent her a hard glance.

He lives! Jazzica thought. *My son lives! So do I, and the Revved-Up Mother. We all live!*

"He has done well, Jazzica," the Revved-Up Mother husked.

14

Jazzica looked at Pall, tried to smile with a generous mouth, said, "Excellent, Pall. You may return to your studies."

"Yes, Mother."

Pall bowed, started to leave.

At that moment an understanding came to him. It was less a concept of clearly-defined clarity than an intuition, a hunch revealed by a kind of inner sight, made visible by a mind-organ his mother had called his *eye for the main chance.*

Lately he had been troubled by the terrible knowledge that his childhood was drawing to a close. Gone would be the days of lackadaisicality of youth. He would soon need to choose a Path. Business, like his father? Gourmet mysticism, like his mother? He did not yet know. But the choice would have to be made— and soon.

He turned to the Revved-Up Mother. "Have many tried to be the Kumkwat Haagendasz?"

"Some," she answered after a turbulence of inner mental thought.

"And none've succeeded?"

"None."

"What happened to them?" Pall asked.

The old woman said, "They went machoola."

Machoola, Pall thought. *It's a word I've not heard.*

"Dead?" Pall asked.

"Worse," she said. "Bankrupt. Out of business."

To those who would be of service: There is a Space-Between, a place not precisely at those places more

15

*commonly explored. Yet though it be not obvious, yet it is
nevertheless of vital importance. It is neither to the Left
nor to the Right, but may be found immediately below the
Center. There. That is it. Now scratch.*

—from "The Mauve'Bib I Knew," by the
Princess Serutan

He was a repulsive man, vile and obese, and he stood
strangling a kitten in the shadows of an office decorated
in poor taste. Nearby, lounging insolently on a thermofax suspensor couch, sat a youth of sixteen, sullen of
eye and round of face. Also present was an older man,
his face wearing an aspect of weariness, his fatigue
caught in the dim light of the westinglobes tuned to the
Soft April Dawnglow frequencies.

"Is it not delicious?" the fat man sighed, tossing
aside the dead cat and giggling with malignity of intent.
"House Agamemnides bound for Doon—Duke Lotto
himself overseeing the preparations for our inevitable
takeover. Am I, the Baron Hardchargin, not clever?
Tell me, my nephew Filp-Rotha—tell me in the presence of that man, Peter De Vries, who by some fluke
bears the name of a humorous writer on Old Earth
from a past millenium. Tell me as we sit here in our
great big castle on the planet Getty Premium, to which
we were exiled after doing something terrible somewhere a few years ago, or something. Am I not smart,
if evil?"

"Very smart, Uncle," said the youth.

Damn him! raged the youth in thought. *He's strangling all the best kittens himself!*

16

"And you, Peter, who're my official Mantan and Character Assassin—do you not admire the guile of I, myself, the Baron Vladimir Har—"

"Admire's too tepid a word, Baron," De Vries said. "And yet—"

"Come, come, Peter," the Baron chid. "Surely there is no flaw in my plan. Review it for the benefit of this lad, Filp-Rotha, my nephew—I being, in fact, his uncle, the Baron Vladimir Hardchargin, who is who I, myself, am."

Peter De Vries shifted position in his verifax seating module and faced the boy. "Your uncle's plan is simple, if treacherous," he began. "He appears to be withdrawing from Arruckus by order of the Emperor, Shaddap IV. Duke Lotto and House Agamemnides shall replace him."

"You should've seen the face of Prince Matchabelli of House Pancakes," the Baron chortled. " 'Why does Shaddap favor Agamemnides,' he kept asking me. Why indeed, nyah ha ha."

"The answer is that your uncle and the Emperor are in collusion," De Vries continued. "You are familiar with the unique characteristics of Arruckus?"

Filp-Rotha nodded. "The Dessert Planet. Its surface is entirely covered with sugar. It's virtually uninhabited except for the cities."

"And the primitive tribes that live on the outskirts of the wilderness," the Mantan added. "The Freedmenmen."

"Filthy scum," the Baron muttered. "I loathe redundant names."

17

"Uncle," Filp-Rotha said. "May I—"

"A - h - h - h - h - h - h - h - h - h - h - h - h - h - h - h - h, my nephew looks impatient," the Baron drawled. "My darling Filp, how will you ever learn to succeed me, when you cannot succeed yourself?"

"Huh?"

"I mean, dear boy, how will you ever learn to replace me, when you—no . . . how will you ever manage to stage me, when you cannot stage manage—no . . ." The Baron sighed, said, "Oh, never mind," and, reaching out a quivering, flabby arm, rang a ma-bell. A slim, youthful-looking servant appeared in the doorway. "Bring us more kittens, Duane," the Baron said. "Then have sent to my chambers two young boys, a pumpkin, and the schnauzer. After this meeting I shall wish to be depraved." The servant bowed and withdrew. The Baron commanded, "Continue Peter."

De Vries said, "Lotto and House Agamemnides'll establish control over Arruckus and organize the management of the planet's one export—with which I'm sure you're familiar."

Filp-Rotha nodded. *Who isn't?* "Beer."

"Exactly. It is found wild all over the planet—in pools, mainly, and in smaller occasional pockets known to the natives as beer-bellies. The plan is to allow Lotto to establish the facilities for bottling and distributing the beer, and then to move in, destroy Lotto, and retake the planet. By then House Agamemnides''ve done all the dirty work with licenses, unions, and so forth."

18

"How can we destroy them?" the youth inquired. "They're pretty strong."

De Vries said, "We have succeeded in suborning the Duke's chief accountant, a man named Oyeah—"

"Impossible!" snapped Filp-Rotha. "He is a certified graduate of the Imperial Institute of Accounting and Broadcasting, not affiliated with any other school or institution. He can't be bought."

The Baron tittered. "We have found his price, my darling Filp. You see, he is not satisfied with being the Duke's chief keeper-of-the-books. He wants to be a standup comedian. We shall be in a position to satisfy that desire."

"We? How?"

The Baron smiled. "Continue, Peter."

De Vries said, "We've instructed Oyeah to—secretly —keep two sets of books. At the proper time, our Emperor will announce an audit of Doon. Oyeah's creative accounting will in due course stand revealed. The Emperor will cry treachery, dismiss the Duke, and reinstate House Hardchargin. We shall then move in with our secret weapon to quell any lingering resistance."

"What secret weapon?"

Here even De Vries allowed himself a wry smile. "We shall have a very special staff of busboys," he said. "They'll wear Hardchargin uniform—yet in reality shall be nothing less than two divisions of Imperial Hardehaurhar."

Filp-Rotha fell silent. "You joke!" he whispered.

"Think of it," the Baron preened. "The Emperor's

19

own crack squad of terrorist-bouncers. No customer in the Empire can resist them. With their help, we shall escort House Agamemnides off Doon and into oblivion. As for that Boni Maroni wife of Lotto's, and her son, well, we shall dispose of them later, in highly creative ways. Then we shall consolidate our hold on Doon, corner the beer market, and with our silent partner convert the entire world into the Imperium's first lounge planet."

"Our—your silent partner—?" Filp-Rotha asked.

"Think, Filp, think! Take it as a clue that the new name of Arruckus'll be 'The Shadvlad Rendezvous.' It scans handsomely, doesn't it?"

"Shadvlad . . . You mean . . . !"

"Precisely. Our Emperor. Shaddap IV himself. Why else loan us his Hardehaurar?"

"And for that he gets a full partnership?"

The Baron clapped his fat, horrible hands. "Bravo, Filp! Peter, is not Filp-Rotha, my nephew, a fitting nephew for I, his uncle, the Ba-"

"The Emperor will also cede to the Baron a full directorship in the interplanetary industrial combine NOAMCHOMSKI," De Vries said. "Presumably you know what the acronym stands for."

The youth nodded, said: "Neutralis Organizational Abba Mercantile Condominium Havatampa Orthonovum Minnehaha Shostakovitch Kategorical Imperative."

"You can see, then, nephew, that the stakes are large," the Baron said. "Not only for me, but for you as well. As my successor."

The boy nodded. *Better keep my mouth shut.*

20

"But come! More kittens." The Baron reached out his gelatinous, unspeakable arm as the servant Duane entered with a basket of the small creatures. A look of disapproval crossed the face of De Vries—a look which the Baron detected.

"Peter, you dislike this practice, eh? Yet you know as well as I that generations of Hardchargins have strangled kittens—this, since the days of the Babalusian Captivity on the planet Babalu 4, when Pope Dalai Islama the Eighth led the Over-the-Counter-Reformation against the combined forces of the Haydn Sikhs, the Perfectly Frank Church of Christ of the Saturday Saints, the Jiu-Jitsu's for Jesus of the Judo-Christian Tradition, and the Ayatollah House Cookies."

He omitted to mention the Maha-Aha sect of the Puss'n Buddhists. "So they have, Baron."

"Then come, Peter," the Baron said with a pout, handing a kitten to De Vries. "Behave like my personal Mantan. Strangle the animal."

"Must I?"

"I'm afraid you must."

The fat old pig, thought Filp-Rotha. He watched impassively as the reluctant De Vries choked the cat, while the Baron giggled. *He's repulsive and corrupt. But hey, what the hell, so'm I. So maybe he's not so bad after all.*

And with that thought the young man's features rent with cruelest laughter.

You have read that Mauve'Bib had no playmates his own age on Cowboydan. Yet have you read that he had

21

wonderful companion-tutors? No, you have not. And why not? Because you spent all last night on the visiphone with your friend Marcie. Now go to your sleeping module and do your homework, and don't you dare come down until I summon you via communinet phaselink.

—from "A Teenager's History of Mauve'Bib," by the Princess Serutan

The boy Pall, dismissed from the presence of the Revved-Up Mother George Cynthia Mohairem after his ordeal with the multicolored cube, brooded in his room. The next day he would, with his family, his retainers, and his braces, board the Guild 'Ighliner and leave Cowboydan forever. Yet his thoughts dwelt not on leave-taking, but on word-having, for the final moments he had spent with the old woman had rendered him troubled of brain.

"You may be the Kumkwat Haagendasz, boy," she had said. "Or, you may be just another duff'r, strutting with pride everytime you fry an egg yolk-whole. We shall see."

"And if I am the Kumkwat Haagendasz?" Pall had asked. "What's in it for me?"

The question had obviously taken her aback. "For you? Why . . . a legacy of over three hundred generations of mouth-watering recipes—"

"I don't need recipes," he had replied. "I'm fifteen. I need . . . something else . . ."

"Need? What can you need? You are the son of a Duke!"

"Bee-eff-dee!" Pall had snapped, surprised at his

22

own boldness, his own impulsiveness, his own sheer *obnoxiousness*. "What good's that? It gets me into Boni Maroni, granted. So I end up as pastry chef for some nouvelle Aldebaran place on Vega 4."

"You mind your manners, boy," the woman had said, sweeping her robes together and exiting the room in a huff. The last thing Pall heard was her muttered, "Spoiled little brat."

Am I? he wondered. Yet his mind seethed with it-wasn't-fair resentment. Other youth had friends their own age—boys with whom to out-hang, girls with whom to around-mess. All he had were adults. Well, perhaps things would be better on Arruckus.

A noise sounded behind him. Without looking up he knew it was Safire Halfwit, his father's Mantan and chief Character Assassin. "Your mother's like a pack of gum—" the man began.

"I know," Pall replied. "Five sticks for a nickel."

Halfwit stopped before the boy and frowned. "What's wrong, lad?" he said, his aged, seamed face a leather sofa on which Time and Care had sat once too often. "These Insult Drills bore you, eh? Then wait and see how bored you are when confronted with an enemy younger and smarter than old Safire, facing Rankout to the death, with no quarter given." He glanced about the room, saw that most of the furniture was gone, shipped to Arruckus. "Glum about the move, is that it?"

"Will Arruckus be dangerous?" Pall said, almost eagerly.

" 'Every place is dangerous to the man who talks to

23

his shirt,' " Safire Halfwit quoted. "Mark ye that for wisdom, boy."

"What about the Freedmenmen?" Pall urged. "What are they like?"

Questions, questions. Halfwit suppressed a smile. *What am I, the Encyclopedophilia Prophylactica?* "A careful people," he said. "Hungry, manic-depressive, overweight. Remember, lad, you speak of a people who've almost never known the pleasures and satisfactions to be had from eating an entree."

"They live on nothing but desserts?"

"Desserts, aye. And, of course, the beer. Also on whatever nutrients they can glean from the creatures that roam the sugars."

"Creatures?" Pall had heard legends, but surely—

"Why, lad, don't tell you've never heard of the giant pretzels."

Then it was true! Tales, he'd thought—the exaggerated ramblings of traders, smugglers, and manufacturers' reps who'd returned to the court on Cowboydan with accounts of enormous animal-snack hybrid creatures a hundred meters high. "There really are such giant pretzels, Safire?"

The Mantan, his cheeks seamed naugahyde, his eyes weatherdulled pools of vinyl latex, nodded. "Great roving things they are," he said. "They say a salt-boulder falling off the back of one of 'em can crush a man."

"Well, whoever that man is, he's a fool!" came a voice from the doorway.

"Gurnsey!" Pall cried with pleasure. For it was

24

Gurnsey Halvah, the Duke's troubadour-jester-torpedo. Hunch of back and wall of eye, Gurnsey lumbered in with his twelve-string rickenbacker slung over his shoulder. This he now took down, and tuned the strings, saying to the Mantan, "What be this bag o' farfel yer makin' fer t'sell the young master, now, Halfwit, eh? With yer tales o' giant pretzels patrolling the sugar hills o' the world called Doon?"

"No bag of farfel, this, Gurnsey," Halfwit said, eyes crinkling with mirth. "You've seen the pretzels yourself."

"Aye, 'tis true," Gurnsey said. To Pall's wide-eyed look of wonder he added, "The adult ones, the full-grown, 'll reach a size as big as this castle. The young ones, the nuggets, stand as high as yer ducal nose, lad. The Freedmenmen call the big ones the Three-Ring Yokes of Madness." He winked. "Why, then, here's a conversation with a twist." Halvah chuckled, nodded, winked, cocked an eye, wiggled an ear, added: "And a salty one a' that!"

Pall smiled, then frowned. He normally enjoyed Gurnsey's company—of all his father's men, Halvah was the one Pall was sure he was smarter than. But today his mood was low, besetting him with a yearn keening. Safire Halfwit noticed his melanchol.

"Something's troubling you, Pall," he probed. "What is it? That is, if you can confide in a couple of broken-down old soldiers who've given blood and brawn for their Duke, the good Lotto."

"Aye, and a lot o' Duke he be, too!" Gurnsey said, chortling. "But stay, lad, here's a tune of our new

25

home . . ." Lifting up the rickenbacker, he struck a chord and sang:

> "O-h-h-h, the girls of Cowboydan
> 'll take it in their hand,
> But we prefer the ladies of Arruckus.
> We bring 'em some tuna on ryes,
> An' a side of Aldebaran fries,
> Then we go an' collect our prize,
> 'Cause we know that they'll perform sexual
>   intercourse with us."

Halvah winked at Pall. "Why d'ye think they call such a tune a lay, eh, boy?" Pall began to laugh, and Halvah smacked him hard across the face. "Keep yer guard up, you young pup, have ye learned nothing from old Gurnsey?"

"And what could any man learn from you, ye gnarled old skrobbnig?"

All turned as Drunken Omaha, the Duke's chief bodyguard, lumbered into the room. *It's getting crowded in here,* Pall thought. *Why aren't these men helping to pack?*

Gurnsey cocked his good eye toward Omaha and said, jestingly, "Why don't ye go and stick yer head in a bucket of kreznum, Omaha?"

"And you the same," retorted the massive, blocky man. The two embraced each other, and the chamber resounded with their comradely backslaps.

"Ah," said Omaha. "What a fine schnagg it is, to serve so noble a tzid, and bear arms with such goodly klormers. Come, Gurnsey! Play us a flotz!"

26

"There'll be plenty of time for that once we're settled on Arruckus," came a well-modulated, commanding voice.

All whirled to see Duke Lotto himself in the doorway. He wore the dark gray jumpsuit and tiny red alligator insignia of House Agamemnides. The three men crowded into Pall's room to accommodate him.

As always, Pall experienced a profound sense of how much his father was *his father,* and not another thing, such as a chair.

The Duke nodded greeting, the weight of his preoccupation a burden that would crush. *I must feign ease,* he thought. *Else betray my disquiet and infect it plague-like among the help.*

"Gentlemen, if you don't mind," he said. "I'd like a few moments with my son."

The three men nodded, took their leave, left.

"Father . . . ?" Pall said when they had gone. "The 'Ighliner—is it really as big as they say?"

The Duke paused; his son was yet a boy. *This is my son,* he thought. *And I? I am his father.* The Duke allowed himself a brief smile. *How very convenient that is.*

"Bigger," he said. "The Schlepping Guild's monopoly on space travel permits it to scale up its operation. Economies of largeness have a way of overcoming the flexibility sacrificed when multi-use options are jettisoned in favor of scale."

"That doesn't make any sense."

This is my son, the Duke thought. *Else I'd slug him for offmouthing thus.*

27

"What I mean is, Pall," he said. "The Schlepping Guild has a monopoly on space travel. They can do anything they want."

"Is that why we live in cold stone castles and do everything as it was done fifteen thousand years ago?" Pall asked. "Do they have a monopoly on everything invented since the Middle Ages on Old Earth?"

Lotto nodded. "Everything except weapons, radio, and small appliances. You learned about the Industrial Revolution, didn't you?"

Pall said, "About six centuries ago, all the people around the Empire revolted. They feared they were in danger of being replaced by machines made from industry. So they destroyed all the . . . technology and stuff."

"Exactly." The Duke's face was an ottoman on which his awesome historic responsibility had for decades put up its feet. "Mankind was plunged into pre-technological chaos. It's taken that long for us to regain what level of development we have today. Our political system now rests on an uneasy concordat—a word which, as I'm sure you know, has something to do with grape jelly, but which somehow also means an agreement."

"Yes," Pall nodded. "But what are the basic elements of our civilization, Father?"

"The Emperor and his Imperial House stand in tenuous counterpoise to the Great Big Houses, of which Agamemnides is one, and the unofficial alliance of the Schlepping Guild and the Boni Maroni," the Duke explained. "It is said that if the Guild, with its

28

superior transportation technology, and the Boni Maroni, with their stores of culinary expertise, could ever agree on a smooth working partnership, there would emerge from that detente a catering service such as the universe has never seen. Unfortunately . . ." Lotto shook his head. "The two groups barely tolerate each other. Well—you know your mother. She's Boni Maroni. Ever try getting her to co-operate on something that isn't her idea? Mur-der!"

Dare I speak thus? Lotto thought suddenly. *The boy is but a boy.* Then he thought sardonically: *A boy, yes—but not too young to begin learning about that damnable enigma that is women.*

"Father, when we take over Doon, and control the bottling of the beer . . . will we be rich?"

The Duke permitted himself a moment's satisfied smile, thinking how cogent that question was. "Relatively speaking," he murmured. "But our enemies will keep us busy trying to defend ourselves. We may end up spending our wealth on arms, and men, and bribes, and direct-mail advertising."

"Which enemies?"

"House Hardchargin, for one. The Baron has made no secret of his desire to destroy us. And the Emperor, Shaddap himself—he fears the respect I command among the Great Big Houses."

"Then why are we going to Arruckus?" Pall asked.

"For what we gain by going," the Duke set forth. "Namely, a thing I call *beer power*. But enough . . ." This talk had drained him. "Finish packing." He strode from the room.

He's no help either, Pall thought with his superior ability to think. *Even if there is wealth to be gained from the move to Doon, it'll all be tied up in the business.*

This realization focussed within him in a sudden sparkflash computation, and in the clear brilliance of that illumination, the boy Pall understood a profoundness. His life, hitherto a child's plaything, devoid of direction—seemingly! Or had there in fact always been a plan—a plan within a plan within a plan (whatever that meant (whatever that meant (whatever that meant)))?—was now encompassed by a terrible purpose. He knew the meaning of the word terrible, and he knew the meaning of the word purpose. And therefore he understood deeply the meaning of "terrible purpose." Unless he, in the solitude of his deeply brain-filled mind, misunderstood this revelation, and was in fact confronted with a "terrible papoose."

What could that mean?

No, it was purpose—and he knew what it meant. Likewise did he know, with resonant clarity and un-dimmed thunderclapping immensity, that his terrible purpose would guide him, will-he nill-he, across time and space itself, practically everywhere. And that purpose knelled the mind of the boy Pall in an echo of the words he had shared with the Revved-Up Mother George Cynthia Mohairem, and with his mother the Lady Jazzica, and with himself.

There's no way out of it, he thought. *I've got to get a job.*

It has become apparent that the Boni Maroni network of advance men and rumor-mongers known as the Mis-

sionaria Phonibalonica was of primary importance in the Arruckus incident. The essence of its work was twofold: By disseminating legend, recipes, and free samples over a staggeringly large area of the known universe, it established in the minds of trillions of people the semi-divine status of the Boni Maroni. It also provided an impartial method of distributing some of the vast stores of government surplus, which in the main consisted of staple grains, meta-plankton, and lamb chops.

—from "The Missionaria Phonibalonica: Propheticus Legitimus or What?" by the Princess Serutan

Lady Jazzica glanced around the high-ceilinged room, noting with scorn its decor and furnishings. She stood in the center of the main drawing room of the Governor's Residence in the capital city of Arrucksack, on the planet Arruckus—new home of House Agamemnides. All around her proceeded the bustle and confusion of moving.

A khaki-suited laborer of the Movingmans' Guild entered. Jazzica detected on his jacket the corporate insignia of the Seven Billion Santini Brothers; she watched as he set down a heavy crate on the floor with a grunt.

"Where ya want the étagère from the media room, O Noble Born?" he asked bluntly.

"Put it over there," she said, indicating with a lift of her regal chin a space along a wall.

"In front o' the paintin'?"

He thumbed toward a piece of art on the wall, evidently left by the Hardchargins. It was a three-dimensional lasbrush copy of an artwork from the past.

31

An image of the original had been enlarged to a size of three meters by four, and lent a semblance of glistening motion by micro-diffraction lenses and a polaroil suspension overlay. With a shudder of fatigue Jazzica recognized the artist Steinberg's map of New York from the cover of the *New Yorker,* an ancient magazine from Old Earth.

Is there nowhere in the universe we can escape that thing? she thought in agony.

"Yes," Jazzica said. "In front of the painting."

The mover positioned the object until the artwork was totally hidden. Jazzica thanked him and he left with a bow.

She knew there was something symbolic in her action of obscuring with her own furniture the art of this castle's previous dwellers. Indeed, there was something symbolic in almost everything she did. She looked around the room with satisfaction—and there was something symbolic in that. She adjusted her long flowing dress—something symbolic. She blew her nose —symbolic. *Oh, why can't we just live like normal people,* she thought.

But her Boni Maroni training was too deep, her commitment to the sisterhood's creed too ingrained, for that sentiment to be left unchallenged. *I am a daughter of the Boni Maroni,* she thought almost automatically. *I exist to serve. Well, first I exist to plan the menu, and cook. Then I exist to serve.*

"'eah, now, Mum, 's somethin' wrong?"

Jazzica whirled. Before her stood a plump old woman in a shapeless gray robe. Her hair was a frizzy brown cloud. But it was her eyes that drew Jazzica's attention: They were those of a Freedmenmen woman, their color a depthless red-on-red.

"I'm called the Shutout Mopes," the old woman said. "I'm at yer service, Mum."

"I'm delighted to meet you, Mopes," Jazzica said coolly. "But you must call me My Lady, not 'Mum.'" Jazzica feigned a small laugh, so useful when speaking to inferiors. "I'm not your mother, you know."

The woman stared wide-eyed at her, took an apprehensive step back, and in a frightened whisper quoted, "*'And she shall be delighted to meet you, and not be your mother.'*" The red of her eyes glowed hot. "The legend is true!" She cast a sly glance at Jazzica, half fearful, half hopeful, half challenging. "Are you the One?"

Jazzica examined her carefully. *Of course!* she thought. *The Missionaria Phonibalonica! Their rumors and gossip have reached even this Godforsaken world! But how to probe her meaning . . . ?*

Cautiously, Jazzica said, "What if I am?"

The old woman leaned back and made a great keening sound of exultation. "Aww-reeeeeeeett!" she cried. "You've brought the chops!"

"Chops . . . ?"

"The lamb chops! The lamb chops!"

What treachery is this? thought Jazzica. *She calls for lamb chops, yet I have brought none . . .*

"I'm sure that's very interesting, Mopes," Jazzica said. "But could you tell me exactly what legend are you referring to?"

"Why, My Lady, the Legend told to us a long time

33

ago by the Great Prophet Phyllis." Mopes looked into the distance and quoted Freedmenmen scripture. "'"Behold,"' said the Prophet. '"For I bring ye tasty gourmet recipes from the kitchens of the Boni Maroni. Eat then these lamb chops, and know that one day a One will come who will bring more."'" She peered suspiciously at Lady Jazzica. "Aren't ye familiar with that one, dearie?"

"Mopes," Jazzica said gently. "I hate to disappoint you. But the Great Prophet Phyllis was decanonized by the Boni Maroni thirty years ago. She's no longer a Great Prophet. Her Legends have been discontinued."

The old woman stared, then turned away with a sudden jerk of her head. She said simply, "No lamb chops?"

"I'm terribly sorry, of course, Mopes. You had your heart set on them so, didn't you."

"Then you're not the One?"

"Not that One, no," Jazzica said, then paused, held a half-breath, said, "But I may be . . . the Other One."

"Aiiiieeee!!" keened the woman. "And have ye brought a son along, then, dearie?"

"I have."

"And is it a moody child, spoiled and willful-like?"

"Well . . ."

"Here!" Mopes suddenly tore open her robe, exposing her brown, wrinkled skin and weathered breasts. "Take the meat of my body! Ye've come to free us—you bein' the Other One, and your boy, who I 'spect's the Laserium al-Dilah'. The Mahdl-T, come to drive us to Paradise at last."

34

Jazzica looked at the woman. *Is this a Freedmenmen thing?* she thought. *Or a crazy-old-woman thing?*

"Cover yourself, Mopes," she said. "Go to my chambers and unpack my clothing, please."

"One other bit o' business, dearie," the old woman said, and reached into her robe and withdrew a small object. This she held out to Jazzica. "I brought it as a gift," she said, then added, "That is, if you know what it is, o'course."

Jazzica cautiously took the object. It was of metal, an oblong about the length of her palm, and appeared to consist of a number of blades and other devices cunningly folded into a single sheath. Its color was of purest Canopan crimson. Jazzica recognized it from her Boni Maroni instruction.

"It's a swysknife," she said.

"Aye, that it is, My Lady," Mopes said. Then, with elaborate nonchalance, as though this entire meeting had had as its purpose the posing of this single question, she asked, "And do ye know what it's used for, then?"

I must be cautious, Jazzica thought. *Delay will count against me, and error may prove fatal. Even guessing could result in my losing points.*

Feigning disdain, she examined the thing. She knew such devices were considered sacred by the Freedmenmen, and that their utility went far beyond the uses of a simple knife. It contained several blades of various sizes, but also a number of tiny tools and beerworking instruments—one of which was for prying open sealed canisters of beer. The ancient word for

35

such a device neatly melded its functional and religious significance. Perhaps—

"This is the key to the church—" she began.

"Aiiiieee!" Mopes cried in ecstasy. "Church key . . . is right!"

"I didn't say church key," Jazzica confessed. "I said key to the church."

The woman shrugged, and began to shuffle toward the doorway. "Close enough." Reaching the entrance, she turned and said quietly, "You're the Other One, all right. Steak for dinner sometime soon, Schmai-gunug be willin'." And she disappeared.

What kind of world is this? Jazzica wondered. The woman's expression—"Take the meat of my body"—disturbed her, affirming the importance of anything that could remotely be construed as an entree here on Arruckus. And what or who was the Laserium al-Dilah'? And that last expression—Schmai-gunug?

Some sort of native religious figure, no doubt. The Missionaria Phonibalonica was always careful to interweave its own Boni Maroni mythology with a planet's indigenous religions. Granted, this sometimes resulted in an awkward syncretism—the lemur-like creatures on Rigel 3 now worshipped a god with the characteristics of a tree-spirit and the body of a macaroon. But its enduring virtue was its essential respect for the rich variety of religious forms found throughout the known universe.

Whoever the Great Prophet Phyllis was, Jazzica thought, *she did her work well.*

Jazzica crossed the large room and entered the

central hallway that led in from the building's entrance. A man was walking briskly toward her down another corridor that led from the Duke's offices. Jazzica recognized the short, brisk form of Oyeah, the ducal accountant. His arms were full of books and papers.

"Are your accommodations adequate, Mr. Oyeah?" she asked.

Adequate, yes, he thought. *Adequate—for treachery!*

"Most comfortable, My Lady," he said with a smile. *I am vile,* he thought. *Playing the affable professional while quietly plotting my client's downfall. But I don't care! Anything—anything! to get into show business.*

"This is a crazy planet," Oyeah said. "I mean it. There's no entrees around here. I went for a walk this morning. Went into a restaurant. I sit down, and there's no silverware on the table. I call the waiter over, I say, 'Hey, there's no silverware.' Waiter says, 'Don't worry about it. We don't have any food, either.' I wanna tell ya—"

"You have come to mock the planet of Arruckus."

It was said as a statement, not a question, and with such a force that both Jazzica and Oyeah looked up, startled. In the center of the entrance foyer stood a man. He was short, rather plump, and clad head to toe in a distinctive white fibrous suit consisting of a loose, baggy, shirt-like garment and equally loose pants, with a ring of elastic around each ankle cuff. A loose hood, part of the shirt, enveloped his head. He strode toward them.

"May not a word be said in jest, when God himself betimes enjoys a good laugh?" Jazzica murmured by way of apology.

37

"God does not laugh when the faithful are insulted," the man said sternly.

"My apologies," Oyeah said. "I was merely trying out some new material. If I have offended—"

"You are the boy's mother," the man said suddenly, turning his piercing gaze on Jazzica. "Word has reached every hootch that you have come. You are the woman who brings the Laserium al-Dilah', the Bright Light of the Italian Love Song." In a single swift motion he swept off the hood, revealing a pudgy face, plump cheeks—and the red-on-red eyes of the Freedmenmen. "I am Spilgard, Nabe of Hootch Grabr." He held out his hand. "May we join our meat."

Jazzica met his gaze steadily. *A Freedmenmen nabe,* she thought. *A tribal chieftain. These people could be powerful allies. I must cultivate him carefully.*

Taking his hand in hers, she said, "I join meat with Spilgard." Then, in a dialect of Varietese she knew to be the native tongue of the sugar tribes of Arruckus, she said, "Sked chitown cinefest preem for fox/indie sci-fi pic."

He started, his eyes narrowing in suspicion, yet revealing impressment. "O'seas b.o. off for yank kid pix, rock flix." He allowed a smile to crease his features. "The legend is fulfilled," he said softly. "'And she shall speak as one of you, yet her companion shall be lame. His material shall be old, and wherever he shall go, even there shall he bomb.'"

"Hold a moment, friend—" protested Oyeah, then caught himself and said, "I mean no disrespect to Spilgard. Truly, I am yet new-arrived on Arruckus, and

38

am unfamiliar with the custom of the place. Why, only yesterday, I was walking abroad about the city of Arrucksack, and I saw a man selling shoes. And the prices he did ask for these shoes were an outrageous thing. 'Friend,' I said, 'give unto me a break! Are you—'"

Ignoring the accountant, Spilgard said to Jazzica, "I will tell my people you have truly come. We have waited long. The boy—but for that, later." He bowed quickly, said: "Steak for dinner sometime soon. Schmai-gunug is generous. Boffo." And with that he drew up his hood, turned on his heel, and walked gravely back through the foyer and out the door.

What sort of man was Duke Lotto Agamemnides? We may say he was a brave man, yet a man who knew the value of caution. We may say he was possessed of a highly refined sense of honor—yet, like all leaders, was he no less capable of acts duplicitous and sleazy. We may say this, we may say that—indeed, we may say anything we want. We may say, for example, that he was not a man at all, but rather a highly evolved bicycle. See? We may say just about anything.

—from "House Agamemnides: Historical Perspectives and Worthless Digressions," by the Princess Serutan

The Arruckusian sun had milkied a depthless expanse of daisy-blooming morning sky lightened darkly to the distant broken horizon when Pall, his father, and Gurnsey Halvah approached the Arrucksack landing field. Waiting for them, standing near a heavy-duty

39

orthodontothopter tended by three Freedmenmen, was Dr. Keynes, official planetologist and liberal economist of the planet Doon.

Keynes watched impassively as the trio approached. They each wore a Freedmenmen sweatsuit he had presented as gifts to Halvah the night before. Keynes still bristled at the memory of that meeting.

"You will address the Duke as 'Sire,' 'my Lord,' or 'Your Dukosity,'" Halvah had said. "A more formal term of address is 'Noble Born.' But mark you well— you must never address him as 'Tony.'"

"And why is that?" Keynes had asked.

"It's not his name. Neither is 'Steve.'"

"What if I call him 'Big Dave' . . . ?"

"Nor 'Big Dave,' either. He'll brook not a dubbing with names that be not his given own, I warrant."

"Very well," Keynes had said, concealing his bitterness.

Never address him as Tony, mayn't I? Keynes now thought. *Not brook it, 'll he? Very well, off-worlders. Issue your orders while you may as to who may and may not be called Tony. But Arruckus has many surprises in store for you.*

As the three crossed the expanse of landing field toward him, Keynes took an opportunity to examine the boy Pall. He carried himself well, for one who so youthfully had so small a number of chronological years in the quantity of the magnitude of his age, Keynes decided. Could he know of the furor that swirled around him? Word had spread to every Freedmenmen village, and beyond. The people of sink and of bled, of graben and of pan, of erg and of eek, of smith and of barney—all spoke of the arrival of the one they called the Mahdl-T, the Laserium al-Dilah'.

His thoughts were interrupted by the arrival of the ducal party.

"Dr. Keynes," the Duke said, after Halvah had made the formal introductions. "I'm told I have you to thank for these sweatsuits. Yet are they really necessary? We go simply on a brief aerial tour of a beer harvesting operation. Surely we shall be safe for that."

How meat-lean they are, Keynes thought with disgust. "Safe, perhaps, my Lord," he said. "But once away from the protection of your residence, you are subject to the natural forces of Doon—the sugars, and beer. You'll find that the beer permeates everything here—and that means calories."

"Hence the sweatsuits, eh?"

He's a smart one, this Duke. "Yes, Sire. They've been perfected by the Freedmenmen over centuries to minimize accumulated body fat. I would be derelict in my duties were I to permit you to travel abroad without them."

"Will we see a pretzel?" Pall asked.

Keynes eyed the boy carefully. *What an intelligent question,* he thought. "Undoubtedly," he replied. "Wherever there is beer harvesting, there are pretzels."

"Why?"

What a marvelously penetrating query, Keynes thought almost against his will. *Perhaps this boy is the Laserium al-Dilah', the Messiah, and the greatest*

41

human being who ever lived. "Pretzels go well with beer," he explained. "As do potato chips, taco chips, and n—other things . . ." He turned to the Duke. "Permit me to adjust your sweatsuit, Your Dukosity."

He was going to say something else, Pall thought. *Could it have been nuts? Yet why not say it?*

"The hood is to be worn in open country," Keynes explained, adjusting the Duke's suit as Halvah watched warily. "These sleeves can be drawn back slightly, to give a more casual, fun appearance, a kind of I'm-ready-for-anything look. The pants have elastic cuffs for a snug, trim fit over socks. I prefer a slight blousiness in the pants, I think it makes for a more airy, playful effect—a sort of Renaissance fluffy concept that I think is really attractive. You can tuck the shirt in or let it stay out. I personally leave mine out, but that's me, I have this sort of crazy thing for shirttails."

"I'll leave mine out, too," the Duke said.

That was wise, Pall thought. *Leaving his shirt out as a token of respect—men would be willing to die for such a leader.*

Keynes turned to Pall, said: "Now let's take a look at—" He stopped and stood back a step, frowning. Presently he said, "You've worn sweatsuits before?"

"This is the first time," Pall said.

"Then someone showed you how to tie the drawstring . . . ?"

"No, I just took a wild guess."

The Freedmenmen guards, who had been idling near the 'thopter, suddenly stood and began to murmur among themselves. One of them cried, "Lasagna Allah

42

Mode!," was slapped in the face by another, who whispered something harshly to him. Then the first one nodded, shrugged, and cried, "Laserium al-Dilah'!"

Keynes whirled, and gave an angry signal to them by drawing his index finger across his throat. He turned back to the boy and his father. "Pay no attention to them," he said. "They're of the native tribes, and like to call out random words in Italo-Arabic from time to time."

But as he shepherded the three aboard the or-thodontothopter, Keynes mulled on words from the legend. *"And he shall tie the drawstring right the first time, and his guess shall be wild."*

Duke Lotto worked the controls, and in a minute the orthodontothopter was airborne, its braces tight, its instruments well-fitted, its rubber bands taut and pulling smoothly. "I told your brewmaster to explore the area southeast of the Shield," Keynes said.

Lotto nodded and banked the 'thopter in that direction. On either side of them, escort 'thopters followed. Presently they were over the Shield, an ultrathin membrane of authentic animal skin that offered full protection to the city while allowing maximum sensitivity.

Pall gazed out the window, aware suddenly that this would be his first full glimpse of the Arruckusian landscape. The terrain immediately surrounding Arrucksack was desolate and flat, extending for many kilometers in all directions. Its color was a deep russet streaked with gold.

"I thought this land'd be white," he said to Keynes. "Or isn't this a sugar area?"

"All of Arruckus is a sugar area," the planetologist said. "But there're different kinds of sugars. This plain's a 70-30 blend of dark and light brown. All the major cities're built on such areas—"

"—because the brown sugars're firmly packed," Pall said. "Of course."

The Mahdl-T will know your world as if he had already lived there during a junior year abroad," went the legend.

Keynes shook his head, then said, "Where we're headed, out into the Great White Way, the ground is trickier—confectioner's pits, bowls, cube ranges. And, of course, the Big Rock Candy Mountains. That's where the white sugar is—and the beer."

"And the pretzels?" Pall asked.

"And the pretzels."

Gurnsey Halvah tuned a string on his rickenbacker, then sang softly:

"Who be the man who wants to roam
Across a field of sugar fine,
Only to be smashed to death and ground into little
    pieces
By a gigantic pretzel?
Not me, O Lord, Aeyah! Hah! Ah-
Yi-yi-yi-yi-haaah! Hayah!
Not me! Ah-yee-yah-yee-yah—"

"Gurnsey—" Lotto interposed, and gave the subtle family hand signals indicating *shut up*.

"Aiyaeah! Hoh!
Not me! Hahah!

44

To walk across the open sugar?
Be crushed by the monster bloody bleeding awful
    pretzel? Do I look
crazy to you, m'Lord? No, thanks! Aiyah! I'll pass!
    Yeeaiah!
Give me a rain che—"

"Gurnsey!" Lotto snapped. The minstrel-bodyguard fell silent.

"Your man enjoys his singing," Keynes commented.
Wish we did, Pall thought.

They flew on, the ground beneath their wings gradually shifting in hue of spectral coloration to a lighter brown, then beige, then shading imperceptibly to white. The flatness of the plain gave way to an undulation of surface, a rollingness of topography. No longer was the ground packed; now the surface was covered by a brilliant snowy dazzle. Wisps of white curled up from gradually-sweeping-upward dunes, and veils of glittering haze curtained the horizon as sugar crystals, borne up by wind and held aloft by currents, reached atmospheric heights and simply hung around.

This was the Great White Way, the vast expanse of white-sugar desert that covered much of Arruckus between the sorbet ice caps at the poles. Pall watched his father bank the 'thopter, saw the escorts respond.

"There," Lotto said, indicating a structure in the distance. What had seemed to be merely another irregularity in the landscape began to take on man-made form. "Is that a beerwagon?"

Keynes peered and nodded. "Big operation," he murmured. "Looks like a fifty-case-a-day-class rig."

Pall saw, growing larger as they approached, a huge platform on caterpillar tracks. Upon it sat a massive tank from which several large hoses snaked out and into the ground. In the air above the beerwagon, three small 'thopters hovered.

"They're looking for pretzelsign," Keynes explained. "The routine is to get in, pump brew as fast as possible, then get out by first pretzelshow. A big carry-on should be nearby to lift the whole operation out of here . . ."

"Could that be pretzelsign?" the Duke said, pointing.

In the distance, about five kilometers from the beerwagon, they saw a low, blunt-topped sugarwave moving slowly across the sugarscape in the direction of the harvester.

This Duke has keen eyesight, Keynes thought. Then he remembered the words of the prophecy: *"And the Mahdl-T's father shall have exceptionally good hearing. As for his eyesight, we don't know. He may wear glasses."*

Even that is consistent with the myth, Keynes thought.

"Good eye, Sire," Keynes said. He took the microphone from the control panel, flicked it on, and said, "This is the ship of Duke Lotto Agamemnides, calling Brew Unit Four. Pretzelsign sighted northeast of your position. Estimated pretzeltime of pretzelcrawl 'til pretzelshow, fourteen minutes, over."

A burst of static came from the radio, then a voice said, "Roger, Sire."

Another voice came over the speaker. "Spotter One calling Brew Unit Four. Pretzelsighting confirmed.

46

Estimated time of pretzelintercept, thirteen and one-half minutes, over."

"Acknowledged, Spotter One," said the voice from the harvester. "Carry-on acknowledge, over."

There was a pause—only static crackled the silence and dead air speakered the ambience.

"Repeat, Carry-on acknowledge, over."

Again only a crackle could be heard.

"Where's the carry-on?" the Duke asked, holding the 'thopter at hover above the beerwagon. The sugarwave of the pretzel drew closer.

"I don't know, Sire," Keynes said. Pall's deep training discerned from Keynes's voice-tones that the man didn't know.

"We're going in to get them," the Duke said suddenly, banking the 'thopter with a sharp veer.

"Brew Unit Four," came a new voice on the speaker. "This is Carry-on Delta Fiver, we read you, are preparing for liftup, over."

Lotto said grimly, "Dr. Keynes, tell them we're going to pick them up. Call off the carry-on."

"But Sire—the carry-on is much larger, and can be here in three minutes—"

"Explain the principles of public relations to the Doctor, Gurnsey," the Duke said. Taking the microphone, he called into it, "Brew Unit Four, this is your Duke, Lotto Agamemnides. I can't tell you how happy I am to be here this afternoon, over."

"His Dukosity wants to win the loyalty of the men," Gurnsey whispered with a wink toward Pall.

"—and just to get things off on the right foot, we're

going to set down fifty meters southwest of your position and lift off your entire crew before the pretzel surfaces, over."

"But what about the harvester?" Keynes protested. "The carry-on has a bay big enough to hold it. All we can do is take the men—we'll lose the equipment!"

"It's insured," murmured the Duke. He broadcast instructions for the carry-on to clear the area and for the beercrew to prepare to abandon the beerwagon.

He's a crafty one, this Agamemnides, thought Keynes.

"The pretzel's picked up speed, m'Lord," Gurnsey Halvah said.

"Right."

The Duke brought the 'thopter in for a landing as his escorts followed suit, the four ships dwarfed by the massive beerwagon. Pall was aware of a tension in the air, a charged feeling, as of static electricity, or acute embarrassment. And the nostrils of his nose were assailed by a pungent yeasty aroma—beer. A deep rumbling seemed to emerge from the landscape itself and dwell in the ears of his head.

"Attention, harvester crew: abandon your facility and board these 'thopters," Lotto commanded into the microphone. "We estimate four minutes to pretzel-show. Move, you scurvy sugardaddies!"

Pall stared rapt as the hatch of the beerwagon dropped open and men began scurrying out. *All this for beer,* he thought. *Beer is the key. It is why these men risk their lives every day out on these wild sugars. It is why we have come here, knowing Arruckus is a trap,*

48

waiting for the Emperor and House Hardchargin to spring. It is the reason the Schlepping Guild is so cautious in its dealings with us.

Yet the entire picture made no sense. Of what use was beer, except for its known libational properties and its mild consciousness-altering effects? And Keynes—he obviously knew more than he was admitting. Was beer the key to him, too? And to the Freedmenmen? And what about ale—

"Quickly, boys, he's almost surfaced! Jump in!"

Gurnsey Halvah had flung open the door to the 'thopter and begun helping several beermen clamber aboard. Outside the air was alive with static charge, and the rumbling had been joined by an unceasing hiss and a sound of hail pelting the ground. *The salt from its back,* Pall thought.

"Secure for takeoff," the Duke snapped, starting the 'thopter's rubber band engines.

"We're overloaded, Sire," Gurnsey said.

"She'll make it," Lotto said grimly, throttling the engines full. The orthodontothopter shook, then slowly lifted. The engines whined, rubber bands straining, appliances shifting against their wires. But the 'thopter gained momentum and was soon airborne, as the three others, equally sluggish, lifted off and joined it in formation.

"Here he comes!" someone cried. Pall craned to see through a window and looked down toward the beerwagon.

The surface of the ground appeared to collapse into a large hole around the wagon. The beerwagon shuddered and began to bounce and vibrate, its hoses flopping uselessly, its treads snapped and flapping like ribbons.

Then Pall saw it.

A mammoth curved thing rose up out of the collapsing hole. Its largeness was extreme; it may have risen two hundred meters above the ground. It was vaguely heart-shaped, its body describing three ring-like segments, one under two, all roughly equivalent in size. Its color was a nicely-baked brown. The central knot, where its length looped around itself, shuddered hideously. At the four and seven o'clock positions its body ended in two overlapping segments attached to the central, bottom ring. One of these was its head; there, its eyes glared with mindless malignancy, and huge jaws yawned a black cave of void into which Pall now watched the beerwagon fall in a slow, dream-like cascade. The other overlap was its tail, a short quivering stub that throbbed. Great boulders of salt rained off the back of the pretzel as in rockslide. The air crackled with static electricity. With a deafening roar the pretzel burrowed back into the ground, and was gone.

That's one of the biggest pretzels I've ever seen, Pall thought.

But his attention was caught by Keynes, who stared with a solemn expression at the hole left by the monster and whispered, "Sugar in the morning, sugar in the evening, sugar at supper-time. Blessed be Schmaigunug and His Baker. Steak for dinner sometime soon. Boffo."

"Boffo," murmured the beermen.

Duke Lotto Agamemnides sat back wearily in the ornate chair at his massive desk. Both pieces of furniture were hewn of true Gnoorweej'n wood, of timbers plucked from the swamp-malls of Nigel-4. Three weeks had passed since the episode of the rescue of the beerworkers—three weeks of court intrigue, rumors of treachery, the apprehension of nine Hardchargin spies, and the poisonings of two minor officials. *Something's terribly wrong,* the Duke thought. *Things are too quiet around here.*

Even the two poisonings were bothersome. One was a classic case of chavez—poison administered in the victim's fruit. The other, equally time-honored, involved chaubakky—toxins secreted in the victim's chewing tobacco. The traditional nature of the two killings disturbed the Duke. It suggested a reaffirmation that in fact there existed between House Agamemnides and House Hardchargin (for the murders could have been perpetrated by no other House) a state of direst kramden.

Lotto smiled sardonically at the thought. Kramden was generally acknowledged to be a somewhat archaic term—"a formal state of feud between two Houses who ought rightly to be best pals." There seemed little hope

51

that the two Houses would be anything to each other but the deadliest of enemies.

A noise at the doorway caused him to look up. "Yes?"

It was Safire Halfwit. The Mantan looked weary, apprehensive. "We have a problem, m'Lord," he said. "The NOAMCHOMSKI audit—the Emperor himself is to conduct it."

"When, Safire?"

"Today. We just received word."

Lotto looked at his adviser. The meaning of the tactic was clear. "So," he said. Halfwit nodded. "Then . . ."

The Mantan nodded again, moved slowly into the room, his aged face creased in calculation, his fingertips pressed in concentration. "Perhaps . . . ?"

"No, Safire, we daren't," Lotto said.

"But the Baron will—"

"What the Baron will, I may," Lotto said firmly, striking the desk with his fist. "What I will, the Baron may or may not—depending on whether I do."

"And if," Halfwit added.

Lotto paused, stunned by this last remark. *Treachery? From Safire? Impossible!* "What do you mean, Safire?"

The Mantan frowned. "My Lord—what do you mean, what do I mean?"

"I mean, man, what do you mean 'and if'? Unless you mean what I think you mean—in which case, I caution you, you play a dangerous game."

Halfwit's eyes widened as he realized the meaning of the Duke's words, or at least thought he did. "My Lord—!"

Lotto nodded grimly. "Precisely."

"Um . . . precisely what, my Lord?"

We are reduced to this, the Duke thought bitterly. *To uncertainty within uncertainty within uncertainty, gambits within gambits within gambits, redundancy within redundancy within redundancy—*

"Let me explain, Sire—"

—within redundancy.

"Sire, when I said 'perhaps,' I was suggesting we use the family atomics to hold the Emperor hostage. Then you just said we daren't, and suggested that the Baron'll ally himself with the other Great Big Houses and kill Shaddap to suit his purposes. Then I said—"

"No, Safire. I thought you were saying we should propose an alliance with the Emperor against the Baron, and bargain with the Schlepping Guild (via our control over the beer) to import microwave disorientation vests from Ix-Nay. I detected treason in the notion, and suspected—"

"No, no, Sire, I meant—"

"Hold." Lotto held up his hand commandingly. "We have conversed in feints and hints, and have got our meanings crossed. From this hour forth, for purposes of war strategy and the highest security, I suggest we speak in complete sentences."

Halfwit allowed a rueful smile to invade the keep that was his face. "Thank goodness, Sire," he said, sinking into the visitor's chair. "One more exchange of 'if' and 'then' and I'd've had to call time out and ask what the hell we were talking about."

A noise from the hallway caught their attention. The doors flew open and an Imperial guard detail marched in. "My Lord Duke Lotto Agamemnides," the captain announced. "His Imperial Stupendousness the Emperor Shaddap IV commands your presence at once."

"I attend his Imperial Unbelievableness with dispatch," Lotto said, obeying the forms. With a worried look to Halfwit, Lotto rose and accompanied the guards.

They moved in the direction of the Agamemnides accounting office. Both the Duke's summons, and the presence of Shaddap himself, promised to bode naught but direst ill.

True, such audits were routine, particularly during a time of Changeover, when one House ceded fiefdom to another. Yet the Emperor had a staff of C.I.A.'s to perform such regular tasks—indeed, Shaddap himself was not a Certified Imperial Accountant, and could at best only oversee the work of a duly accredited representative of the Bookkeepers' Guild.

They are making their move, Lotto thought. *Now it begins.*

The detail led him to the office and announced him. Inside, Shaddap sat at the Chief Accountant's desk, scowling over two large ledgers. To his left stood Oyeah. The I.I.A.B. graduate looked pale; his eyes could not meet the Duke's.

"Your Superbitude," Lotto said, bowing crisply. As per the accepted procedure, he recited, "My books are open to your eyes. May their balance find—"

"Spare me your pleasantries, my Lord Duke," Shaddap said curtly. "And be so kind as to explain this most interesting phenomenon before me. What should

54

properly be a single accounts ledger has, under the ministrations of Accountant Oyeah, spawned a twin. Yet it is an exceedingly unidentical twin."

"You mean, Your Ineffability—"

"I mean, my Lord Duke, that with one hand you play the trustworthy administrator of the beer commerce of Arruckus, yet with the other you have been skimming the cream and using it to line your own pocket!"

Lotto addressed Oyeah. "Can you . . ."—there was no other way to put it—". . . account for this, sir?"

"I was . . . merely obeying your orders, m'Lord," Oyeah muttered, looking away.

"I see." Lotto strode two steps into the room and pointed his finger at Oyeah. "Treason!" he cried. "Treachery! I'll sue you from here to Cygnus X-1! You'll never work in the known universe again!"

"Guards!" the Emperor commanded, pointing to the Duke. "Indict that man!"

"To your attorneys, House Agamemnides!"

Confusion and litigation exploded in the room. The Emperor's detachment seized the Duke, as a phalanx of Agamemnides soldiers, lawyers, and paralegal girls working part-time to put their husbands through law school burst in. The last thing Lotto saw before a blow to his head robbed him of consciousness, was the satisfied smirk of the Emperor as he nodded toward the tight-lipped Oyeah, and slammed shut the two ledgers.

It is the nature of greed to want what it does not have. Thus is it eternally unsatisfied. This the Baron Vladimir Hardchargin doubtless knew. Why, then, did he glory in his greed, rather than renounce it in favor of a path more likely to bring contentment? Because he was a fat pig.

—from "My Own Personal Theory About the Arruckus Incident, In Case Anybody Wants to Know," by the Princess Serutan

The Baron Vladimir Hardchargin drifted haltingly across the entrance foyer of the Governor's Residence in Arrucksack. Excelon suspensor jets supported the main of his fatso bulk as he nodded gigglingly with satisfaction. The forces of House Agamemnides were routed. Arruckus was his.

"Was I not right, Peter?" he asked his Mantan, who moved with melancholy air beside him. "Lotto in custody and bound over for arraignment, his Boni Maroni wife helpless, the boy likewise in our hands—and all thanks to me (the Baron Vladimir Hardchargin), and my skillful use of Oyeah."

"You, and the Emperor's legions of Hardehaurhar," De Vries said dryly.

"Yes, yes, quite right," the Baron said, positioning himself on a nearby throne. "They played their part to perfection."

De Vries shuddered at the memory. Twenty thousand of the Emperor's fanatical terrorist-bouncers had descended on the city of Arrucksack, disguised as a convention of Shriners from the Benevolent Planetary Order of Elkoids. At the fatal hour they had thrown off their fezzes and attacked.

House Agamemnides had been powerless against them. De Vries himself had been present when ten

56

Hardehaurhar had seized an entire division of Agamemnides employees by the scruff of the neck, dragged them to the outskirts of the city, and with a brutal shove sneered, "Don't you think you've had enough for one night, chief?"

Now Lotto was surely defeated: Safire Halfwit was disgraced, fatally embarassed; Drunken Omaha and Gurnsey Halvah were in hiding; the Lady Jazzica and her son were, no doubt, about to be banished, or worse.

"But come, Peter!" the Baron said. "You look glum! Come share with me the pleasure I, the Baron Vl-"

"The Lady Jazzica," intoned a guard.

Two guards escorted her in. She wore a long flowing white robe, her hair pulled back severely. The Baron noted her generous mouth, her magnanimous eyes, her penny-pinching nose, her philanthropic ears.

The Baron smiled. "A-h-h-h-h-h-h-h-h-h-h-h-"

"What do you want of me, Baron?" the Lady Jazzica demanded.

"-h-h-h-h-h-h-h-h-h-h-h-h-h-h-h-h-h-h-h-h-h-h- h-h-h-h-h-h . . ." the Baron said, then stopped, panting, to catch his breath. "The Lady Jazzica. Winner of the Boni Maroni Interplanetary Chicken Festival of 10,173—"

Jazzica detected the clue-tones in his voice, revealing to her deepest levels of awareness that he got the date wrong. "'74."

"Of course. Seventy-four." His plump-faced look of affability suddenly vanished. "Where is your sisterhood of cooks now, eh? All your precious knowledge about well-greased pans is as nothing compared to my small bit of wisdom concerning a well-greased palm." The Baron made a face of grudging admiration. "Somebody write that down. It's not half bad."

"You have prevailed—for now," Jazzica conceded. "But the universe is large, and time is long."

"Do tell."

"For space is infinite, and matter an illusion."

"You don't say."

"Desire is a phantom, satisfaction a mirage."

"Sez you."

"Avarice is a disease, and it is always fatal."

"Your father's moustache," the Baron said, then commanded the captain of his guards, "Take her and the boy. Give the pretzels them."

The man hesitated. "Are you sure, my Lord—?"

"Do you dare question my command?"

"No, my Lord Baron." He bowed, then signalled to an underling. "Bring in the boy."

Pall! Jazzica thought. *Alive!*

She shook her head, breathed slowly in accordance with the Boni Maroni beat-stress, win-with-aerobics exercises.

A pair of guards marched into a nearby hall, re-emerged holding Pall by either arm. He was bound and gagged. Jazzica permitted herself to faint with relief for a few seconds.

The captain nodded to a guard, who strode off toward the kitchen. The Baron observed this with irritation. "Captain, is this necessary?"

Puzzled, the captain replied, "I . . . but obey your command, my Lord."

58

"My command was—"

The guard returned from the kitchen bearing a hand tray. Jazzica strained to identify the round object upon it. *Torture?* she thought frantically. *Here? They wouldn't dare!*

At the captain's nod, Pall was dragged to stand beside Jazzica. The guard from the kitchen brought the tray over to them and stood immobile. Upon the tray was a wicker basket. It was filled with small brown sticks—pretzel sticks, lightly salted.

"Here," said the captain sternly.

Jazzica shook her head mute. Pall, his mouth covered by the gag, likewise declined.

"Captain," the Baron said slowly. "Do you mock me?"

"I, my Lord?" the man said nervously. "I merely obey my Lord's command. My Lord commands, Give them pretzels, and so I—"

"Not 'give them pretzels,' you idiot!" the Baron raged. "Give them TO the pretzels! TO the pretzels! The big ones! In the wilds!" With a strangled gurgle he lashed out with a chubby hand, batted the basket into the air, sent the brown sticks flying. "Why would I, the Baron Vladimir Hardchargin, engineer the most spectacular and devious overthrow of a Great Big House in the history of the Imperium, and then offer to the wife and son of my mortal enemy a basket of between-meal treats?!"

The guard burned bright red, could barely mutter, "As a consolation prize, my Lord . . . ?"

"GET OUT! And take these two to the sugars!"

The captain nodded, bowed, and ordered his guards

to escort the Lady Jazzica and Pall out. The Baron signalled an aide, sighed wearily, and said, "Bring me the accountant."

The soldier disappeared into an adjacent room, and a moment later emerged with Oyeah. The transformation of the Imperial Institute of Accounting and Broadcasting graduate was astounding: he had doffed his official accountant's three-piece robes and wing-tip sandals, and now wore trousers fashioned of Rigelian clam leather, an open-necked shirt of leonard-silk, and hand-made shoes cobbled by the hand-dwarfs of Milanos-2.

"Baron!" he said with jaunty demeanor. "You look good, kid. Really."

"Thank you," the Baron said softly. "You certainly wasted no time in preparing for your new career, Oyeah."

"No, I mean it." Oyeah turned to De Vries and, indicating the Baron, said, "I love this guy. 's the only guy I ever saw needs a null-grav field from Ix-Nay just to stand up. Fat? Come on! The Schlepping Guild pays him *not* to fly!"

"Very amusing, Oyeah," the Baron said.

"Hey, thanks. So when's the run?"

"The . . . run?"

"The gig, man. When do I open?"

"A-h-h-h-h-h-h-h-h-h-h-h-h, yes. Why, as soon as you're ready. As soon as you've packed."

Oyeah looked suddenly worried. "Packed? What packed? I'm here! This must be the place, right?" He smote his forehead with an open palm, tried to swallow

60

in a dry throat. "Hey, I get it. No problem. You need me to clear out for a few days to remodel the room. I can dig it. Hey—the room? The whole planet! Am I right?"

"You are wrong, Oyeah," the Baron sighed. "You will indeed commence a 'run'—in the cafeteria of the Main Detention Facility on the prison planet Salacia Simplicissimus." The Baron chuckled. "Talk about a captive audience . . ."

The accountant's face drained white. "But you said—"

"People say a lot of things in this business," the Baron replied with a dismissive wave of his pudgy hand. "Next time, get it in writing."

Two burly guards seized Oyeah and dragged him away. As the Baron chortled and signalled for food, De Vries looked at him solemnly.

"He'll go to the Comedians' Guild," De Vries said.

"Let him," came the reply. "We control the beer now, Peter. Think on it! All that remains is to decorate the planet and install the booths. The Shadvlad Rendezvous will be a reality in less than six months."

"What about the Freedmenmen?" the Mantan asked bluntly. "They'll not stand idly by—"

"The sugar scum? We may ignore them. They don't go to night clubs anyway." He signalled an aide. "Bring me the architect. I have some sketches of my own I want him to incorporate in his scheme for the main lounge."

"Is that wise?" De Vries asked. "You hired him—"

"I hired him to please me, Peter," the Baron said.

61

"Am I not the client? And is the client not the boss? But enough." He reached out a flabby arm and produced a thick binder. "Come look at these swatches. Did you ever in your wildest imaginings think there could be so many different types of black velvet?"

O Cowboydan, world of several places,
Planet of some large objects,
Where is your glory, if you're so
Great?
Now Arruckus, now, there's a planet—
Things happen, events exciting.
Action, adventure, romance, intrigue.
Let us go, then, you and I,
Aboard that big silver bird up in the sky,
To Doon, to Doon, to Doon, to Doon,
To Doon, to Doon, to Doon, to Doon.
As our caissons go rolling along.

— from "Hymns, Prayers, and Show Tunes of
Mauve'Bib," compiled by the Princess Serutan

The Lady Jazzica, her hands tied behind her and her mouth gagged, struggled to adjust her position in the orthodontothopter. Beside her, Pall lay similarly bound, but without a gag.

"Eh, Skagg, look a' tha' 'un wiggle," rasped one of the two guards, a stocky thug named Krudd.

His companion, piloting the craft, guffawed. "Wot a pity if'n we let 'er go 'thout a li'l fun, eh mate?"

Jazzica sought to calm herself. They had been loaded onto the 'thopter after their audience with the Baron. She was certain their fate was to be killed, then left for

62

the pretzels to destroy. *These poor fools,* she thought, glancing at her captors. *They themselves'll surely be killed when they return. The Baron wants no witnesses. Then whoever kills them'll be killed too. Then the killers of the killers'll be killed, and so on, until no one in the universe'll be left alive.* The import of the thought sent her sensorum reeling. *That'd be terrible!*

"Aye," the one called Krudd said. "'ere, now, Skagg. You fly the bird a bit an' I'll 'ave a li'l fun. Then we'll switch. 'ow's 'at, then?"

"Waw," the other replied with a grunt. "'f you 'ave all the fun first, there won't be any left f'me, innit?"

"Kah-mawn, Skagg—I won' use up alla fun. I'll leave you a bi', now, there's a good lad." He turned his attention toward Jazzica, said with a rheumy-eyed leer, "'ere, then, Miss—d'you come 'ere often?"

Jazzica shook her head. Outside the window she could see they were flying over the Shield, heading for open sugar country.

"Right," Krudd said with leering satisfaction. "'ere, then—wot's a nice bit like you doin' inna place like this?" Then he turned to the man piloting the 'thopter, slapped his knee, and chortled, "'ey, this is fun!"

I'd best humor him, Jazzica thought. She spoke; the gag impeded her mouth movements, resulting in making her answer a foreign, indecipherable thing: "Unh-unh-uhnnah-uhn-uhn."

"Get—" Pall said, then swallowed in a dry throat.

He's trying to use the Cook-Voice! Jazzica thought.

It was a Boni Maroni thing, a technique she had taken pains to teach him.

63

"Each human," she had said as he had listened wide-eyed, "has a specific sonic range of tolerance for voice communication. Study carefully all you meet. You will learn to focus on the narrow range-spectrum of susceptibility in each individual. By pitching your voice to that precise frequency, you will be able to—"

"—make anyone do what I want?" he asked with a child's eagerness.

She had permitted herself to smile. "No, Pall. But the race-instinct of every human being compels him to want to snoop in the kitchen while you're cooking. To look in pots, take little tastes, and use your cutting board for making gin and tonics while you would see to adequate food preparation."

He had nodded solemnly—a boy, yet already displaying a man's stoicism in the face of the cruelty implacable of life's truths.

"By mastering the Cook-Voice, you may irritate, and thereby banish, anyone you choose." Then she'd paused, her mind a galloping boil of doubt.

Dare I reveal to him the esoteric technique? she brutally introspected. But he was heir to her genetic bequeathment, and to that of the Duke. Who, if not he, deserved inheritance of the legacy?

"Now, repeat after me, in this precise tone," she'd instructed. " 'Get *out* of the kitchen. It'll be ready when it's ready.' "

"Get out of the kitchen," he'd attempted. "It'll be ready soon."

"Again. And do not omit the second 'ready.' "

He had applied himself to the study with a single-mindedness and focus of attention worthy of a monk of the sect of the Organized Confucians. One day he had surprised his father during a high-level staff meeting in the Great Hall. Wandering in amongst the assembled officers and aides, he had suddenly whined, "Get *out* of the kitchen, Lotto. It'll be ready when it's ready."

A silence had fallen; men exchanged sharp glances dense with piercing meaning. There had been something so annoying, so irritating, so enragingly nasal in the boy's bitch-tone.

Then Lotto had stood up, said, "My son learns the Boni Maroni Ways and Means. It is good." To Pall he had said, "Remind me to give your mother a raise."

Now, Jazzica realized, Pall was attempting the Cook-Voice with these two henchmen. Would it work?

"'ere, now, lad," the one called Krudd said to Pall. "'ow can I 'ave any fun wi' you talkin' a' me?" He reached his hand out toward Jazzica's dress and slid it under, up her legs.

Carefully pitching his voice, Pall said briskly, "Get *out* of the kitchen."

"'eh? Wot?"

"It'll be ready when it's ready," Pall said.

"Cor, don' like 'is voice much," muttered the pilot, Skagg.

"Get *out* of the kitchen!" Pall said more harshly, and watched impassively as the two men winced. Krudd withdrew from Jazzica and clamped both hands over his ears. "Stop! Stop!" he cried.

"It'll be ready when it's ready!"

The 'thopter took a sudden dip as Skagg, shaking his

head in agony, cried, "I'll set 'er down 'ere! Let's dump 'em! Anythin' t' stop that 'orrible sound!"

Krudd nodded, stared fearfully at Pall.

"Untie her," Pall said.

The man looked doubtful, said: "Cor, dunno, lad. We've orders to—"

"Get *out* of the kitchen!"

"There there, lad. There, there . . ." Hastily he untied Jazzica's hands, removed her gag, untied Pall's hands. In a moment the 'thopter touched down on a stretch of flat white sugar and rolled to halt.

Pall opened the hatch and prepared to leap out. Jazzica looked at the two men. "Give us your knives and canteens," she said.

Skagg said anxiously, "O, we couldn', Milady. 'f we 'ave to explain back at the base where they went, we'll get in a peck o' trouble—"

Jazzica called on her years of experience to pitch her Cook-Voice to its most devastating whininess, said: "How can I *make* your *dinner* if you get in the *way* all the time?"

"'ere!" Skagg cried, shoving toward her two knives, two canteens, and a complete Freedmenmen kit for surviving on open sugars. "Jus' go—and to hell with ye! I'd like t'see you try usin' that voice wi' the pretzels . . ."

Pall leaped out of the 'thopter, found footing on the sugars, and helped his mother out. They stood back as the craft took off. In a minute it was but a speck on the horizon, then was gone.

They stood still amid the silence in the vastness of the

Great White Way. Each small step produced an abrasive rustle, as below their feet loose topsugars shifted and crunched. The land was slightly rolling, with occasional rock-candy outcroppings to punctuate the eye's reading of the terrain's sentence. Above, the Arruckusian moons hovered in twin orbs of icy white, paired after-dinner mints set in a field of glittering silver-blue jimmies.

"What about pretzels . . . ?" Jazzica breathed.

"We're safe for now," Pall said bluntly.

"Poor Lotto—"

"He's fired. Either that, or laid off." Pall sneered. "Small difference."

She stared at him. His tone—so cold! So brutally frank! "Pall—!"

"In any event, we're on our own," Pall said. "I see it all now. Oyeah cooked the books, left an opening for the Emperor and NOAMCHOMSKI to oust Father and reinstate the Baron. Probably brought in Hardehaurhar disguised as Shriners. Drunken and Gurnsey are in hiding. Safire Halfwit is fatally embarrassed. Now the Baron sits in Arrucksack, waiting to hand over Arruckus to Filp-Rotha, his nephew. The Guild won't squawk —they care only about beer. All we have on our side is the Freedmenmen—the weirdest people in the galaxy."

"Pall!" she hissed. "How can you . . . know these things?"

"Just a hunch."

Pall stared off into the distance. Thoughts raced each other through his mind.

What mattered now was survival. His parents had

grown up in their world—but their world was gone. With his father ruined, whatever inheritance Pall could have looked forward to was moot. The usual professions for young people like him—as lawyers, investment bankers, financial counselors, pension fund managers—would now never be. He was stuck on this crappy sugar-covered planet, with no academic degree, no chance to get into a decent college, and no connections. His training as a cook was next to useless on a world devoid of entrees. He had his mother to look after. He was barely fifteen, and his life was an over-and-done-with thing.

"Wait a minute," he murmured. "The beer . . ."

"Pall—!" his mother said, understanding everything.

"You understand everything, Mother?" he said savagely. "We must find the Freedmenmen. They control the beer. If we can control them, we can do business with everyone—the Emperor, the Guild, everyone."

"Control them?" Jazzica asked, jarred at the deepest levels of awareness by a monstrous hint-implication suggested by her son's talk-words. "How?"

"I don't know yet," Pall said. "We'll have to join them first."

Jazzica stared. *Could it be?* she thought. *That strange and savage people, the Freedmenmen—is it truly necessary we ally ourselves with them? To live as they live, dress as they dress, survive on nothing but beer and pretzels and desserts until we, like they, end up red-eyed and disgusting and FAT—!*

"NO!" she cried. "It . . . must not be!"

"Be quiet," Pall said. And Jazzica was shocked by

68

the man-tones and shut-up harmonics in his voice. "We've no alternative. They already think me the Mahdl-T. Very well—there's a start in that. But it's an insufficient thing . . ."

Jazzica felt fearful of the cold precision of his being, yet could not but query, "But what if it turns out that you're not their Mahdl-T? What if you're only our Kumkwat Haagendasz?"

"I don't know!" he cried. Whirling on her, his eyes raged wild. "I don't know if I am the Kumkwat Haagendasz or not! I have no idea what the Kumkwat Haagendasz *is!*"

Jazzica stared at him. Scare-raspings of skin terror clawed along her epidermis. Tiny needle-pointings of not-knowing-what-to-think dread echoed somewhere in her mind. Somewhere within her generous mouth she tried to swallow in a dry throat. "Neither do I," she at last confessed.

"You don't!"

"No," she stammered. "All my Boni Maroni teachers referred to it as if we all knew its meaning."

"And no one did?"

"No . . . Pall." She looked away, abashed. "I think it has something to do with being able to prepare many dishes so they all end up being ready at the same time—"

"Be quiet."

Pall turned away, suddenly absorbed in the capacity of his mind for *calculation*. The inflow of data proceeded steadily, inexorably, and the computations that arose from it fed back into the system. He was vaulting

69

up notches of awareness in the levels of his conscious apprehension, yet he was also *not subsumed* by those very streamings of thought. He was therefore able to know, at that precise instant, that what he was engaged in at that moment was called *thinking,* and the climax-resolution-solution process that seemed so ineffable was in reality nothing more—or less—than *having an idea.*

"—that maybe even the Revved-Up Mothers don't know what the Kumkwat Haagendasz is," his mother was saying.

He whirled to face her.

"It doesn't matter," Pall said. He rose and clambered atop a small rock-candy ledge, held his arms out and intoned to the entire Great White Way, ghostly in the moonlight: "It doesn't matter! All that matters is, I have a great idea!"

He leaped down and confronted her, wild-eyed, his eyes burning with an inner great-idea-having-fire. "I have need of a job, Mother. And the Freedmenmen can give it to me. We must find them. We'll tell them I *am* the Kumkwat Haagendasz. Since no one knows what it is, no one's to say it isn't me."

Pall saw it all in that stopped instant of mental imagining. The Missionaria Phonibalonica had been here. Pall's claim at Kumkwat Haagendaszitude would be credited. From that would emerge the necessary thing—what his father had called *beer power.*

And Pall felt a great peace suddenly blossom within himself. The question that had plagued him since the

70

moving day on Cowboydan had been answered. He sagged, fell to his knees, and felt tears streaming from his eyes and coursing down his youthful cheeks. He lifted his face to the twin moons of his new homeworld. "Father!" he cried. "I have a career!"

book two

MAUVE'BIB

———————————————————————————————

Many have remarked on the rapidity with which Mauve'Bib came to proclaim himself the Laserium al-Dilah'. For them, let us say that, to him, religion and business were one. As Mauve'Bib himself said, "God does not care what you do, or why you do it. What is of importance is that you keep accurate records, and can produce all pertinent receipts."

—from "Mauve'Bib: The Collected Press Conferences," edited by the Princess Serutan.

Jazzica awoke at first daylight, the dim glow of skydawn feathering chocolate-chip-mint-ice-cream-green colored streaks in the still of the night beyond the blue horizon. She sat up in the sweat-tent and glanced about. Her Boni Maroni training, coupled with the vision she could create by looking with her eyes, disclosed an optic datum: the absence of her son meant that he was not there.

The heat of the sweat-tent was a stifling thing, and Jazzica allowed herself to permit herself to detect in herself the preliminary throat-yearnings of thirst. Probing with the superior sensitivity refined by deep training, she felt want-cravings for a liquid, something preferably cold, and light, crisp and satisfying time after refreshing time—

A beer would spot-hit right about now, she thought.

"You're up," said a voice, and Pall unzipped the tent's entrance and leaned in. "Good. We must move. Here. Eat this and put these on."

She noted the clue-tones of brat-bossiness in his speech. "All right . . . Pall," she hoarsed.

75

She ate the C-biscuit he had handed her, and regarded the garment he thrust into her hyperaware hands. Both pieces were of a soft fibrous material, bright yellow. The trousers appeared to fasten by way of a drawstring threaded around the waist. The shirt, blousy and soft, bore a stencilled design on its front. Jazzica held up the shirt and read: STOLEN FROM THE ATHLETIC DEPARTMENT, CRAB NEBULA A&M.

"It's a Freedmenmen sweatsuit," Pall said, gathering together the items he had examined the previous night from the Freedkit given them by the killers Skagg and Krudd. "Helps you sweat off excess calories gained from the sugars and the beer."

"Will it fit—?"

"One size fits all."

How remarkably adult that observation, she thought, donning the garment. *He is indeed no longer a child. He is a teenager.*

They emerged from the tent and Pall collapsed it, adding its folded form to the gathering of other instruments and gear from the Freedkit pack. A sheet of beerpaper fluttered to the ground; Pall unfolded it and read an inventory of the kit's contents: "Lennonjons, sweat-tent, sweatsuit, beermug, snorkplug, flamtap, filtcig, lumpers, chiksoop with krep-lock, brewer hooks, ferndoc, caltrans, link-ray, cal-ripkin sac-fly . . ." He looked up at his mother. "A bespeakment of great technical sophistication's in all this gear-crap."

She had never heard such harsh control in him

76

before. Shuddering at the cold implacability of every-thing, she husked, "Yes."

He pointed to a range of mountains rimming the horizon in the distance. "Let's go. There. We'll travel by day, stay close to these rock-candy outcroppings. We must move like the Freedmenmen do, in irregular rhythm, so as not to attract the pretzels. Walk this way."

"If I could walk that way, I wouldn't need the corn starch," Jazzica said.

"What, Mother?"

He has much yet to learn, she thought. *And there is so little time.*

"Nothing, Pall," she said. "An ancient punchline of wisdom. Let's go."

They set off at a lurching pace. Jazzica watched with admiration as Pall discovered, with a seeming natural grace, the Freedmenmen stride. Step . . . step . . . step-step-step . . . step . . . step . . . step-step-step . . ."

"You walk divinely, Son," Jazzica murmured, fol-lowed.

They walked for an hour. Around them the land-scape was a subtly shifting thing. Sugar whites stretched flat far out to heat-shimmered air in an unbroken-up-by-anything-tall expanse. A rock-candy ridge loomed, came closer with their progress.

Presently they stopped at a broad pond-like pool of whiter-than-white powder. It was a confectioner's pit, one of many depressions in the Great White Way in which windblow and sugarshift had deposited an especially fine sugar—a dust that could suck like quicksand if crossed by the unwary.

Pall signalled for his mother to stop and gently approached the siltfine surface. His instinct was sure: anchoring on his left foot and balancing poised over the talclike pulverate, testingly he put his right foot in. He pulled his right foot out. He put his right foot in and he shook it all about. Then he did the *hoki-poki* and he turned himself around.

That's what it's all about, thought Jazzica grimly.

A new sound could now be audibly heard, a deep rasping from no one particular direction, an abrasive slithering. Pall met Jazzica's gaze.

"Pretzel," he said. Then he smelled the pungent, yeasty aroma of beer. What was the connection between the pretzels and the beer? Keynes had said—but there was no time for such speculation now.

"We've got to reach that outcropping," Pall said, grabbing the pack. "Run!"

He grasped his mother's arm and led her across a flat, around the confectioner's pit, toward an escarpment of rock candy. The rasping grew louder, and Jazzica could feel a shuddering in the ground through her bally-shoes.

"Faster!" Pall shouted.

"I . . . can't," she said, husking roughly in a trouble-muffled voice.

They ran on, the rock candy about a hundred meters away. The ground shook violently, the sharp beersmell a loudyell in their nosenostrils.

The loose sugar dragged at their feet, muttered a

78

snowy crunch with every step. Then it tapered off, as they reached a hard-packed flat surface that led up to the base of the ridge.

"Bop! Bop! Boppa-dop-dop-dop Bop-a-dop Bop!"

"Bongo wafer!" Pall hissed.

The ground now vibrated like a stretched drumskin, as tons of hardpacked sugar formed a single taut membrane, the sugar crystals linked and fused on the molecular level by eons of climatic change. Every step now produced a resonant bongo-bop, adding to the swirling aural frenzy and making of their desperate crossing a Tito Puente thing.

"Faster!" Pall urged.

He seized his mother's hand and they ran across the bongo wafer, their steps producing a clatter of percussive reports.

"Bop! Bop! Ya-bopitty-bopitty-bah-DAH-bop!"

The noise from the pretzel suddenly changed, its deep rumble giving way to a higher-pitched fusillade of cracks.

They stopped, turned to look.

A hundred meters behind them, the ground rose in a sharp-angled peak and snapped in two, like a baked thing.

Shards and pieces of the ruptured bongo wafer fell in a clattering shower as up from the fissure rose a toast-brown hump. Rough white saltrocks clung to its shiny surface.

It reared up higher and higher, finally exposing its stubby head, protruding from the huge hoop-like body.

Two vacant, burning eyes stared at Pall and Jazzica

with primeval hatred, the ancient response every pretzel would show those who would intrude on its territorial realm.

Its mouth opened, spewing beersmell and pretzelbreath in their disbelieving personfaces.

"It's . . . big," Jazzica whispered.

"Yes."

Pall grabbed her wrist and dragged her across the remaining stretch of bongo wafer. The wafer, its percussive integrity now ruptured by the pretzel's emergence, had lost its tension, was easier to traverse. Here was motion their muscles could understand. Here was rhythm. Here was freedom. Here was action, and excitement, and a whole new way to run from a giant man-eating pretzel.

Pall and Jazzica were able to reach the rock-candy ridge quickly.

The pretzel drove blindly at them, slicing through the shattering bongo wafer like an ice cutter. Saltrocks showered from its back onto the flat white surface in a cascade of white falling on top of white.

Pall reached the ridge and saw a narrow crevasse; he guided his mother into it and followed. It was wide enough to accommodate them side by side, and they turned to watch their pursuer.

The pretzel ground its way to the ridge and towered over them, focussed on their location but unable to reach them in their niche. It growled and seemed to rock back and forth on its round belly-segment, stubhead turning left and right in hideous slow motion.

Now are we the hunted, and the pretzel the hunter, thought Jazzica. *Now are we the snack, and the pretzel the snacker. Now are we the crisp, tasty, savory treat for those special times when you want something light but satisfying, or for any old time—*

"Listen!"

Beneath the roar of the pretzel and the crunch of the ruptured ground, they heard a steady bassnote.

"Lump! Lump! Lump! Lump!"

"A lumper!" Pall hissed. "A Freedmenmen device used to attract pretzels. There are people nearby!"

"Lump! Lump!"

The pretzel stopped its rampage and seemed to pause, hovering above them, hesitating. Then it wheeled in a grinding crunch of sugar and set off toward the sound.

In a few moments it was gone.

Pall sent Jazzica a glance.

"Someone planted that lumper," he said. "Who?"

"Freedmenmen," she said.

"Maybe we can find them," he said. "Then I can give them some song and dance about—"

"We have our own forms of indigenous folkloric entertainment."

It was a deep masculine voice crushing like a boot Pall's rash words. It came from above them.

Pall whirled and looked up. Staring down at them from atop the rock candy formation was a short, pudgy man in a sweatsuit. Other figures, similarly clad, stood nearby.

Jazzica gasped.

More men in sweatsuits emerged from the shadows of the rock candy. All had the distinctive red-on-red eyes that told of addiction to beer.

"Time's meat, Spil," one of them growled. "Let's take their packs and be gone."

Pall froze, his mind working methodically. He struggled to suppress fear, felt his body and his mind run through the yogi-bear/yogi-berra relaxation exercises. Once settled into that semi-poised state, he could whip-snap his muscles, lash out, and reach for his wallet to offer them a little something in exchange for looking the other way.

He was too late. The leader leapt down off the higher ledge and approached them. Pall felt fear return. They were surrounded by Freedmenmen in a strange place, with no bodyguards, no weapons, no lawyers. And all this tribe of nomads seemed intent on was the entrees in their packs.

> *Like all creation myths, that of the Freedmenmen is unnecessarily complicated. Yet from it we may learn much, for myth is truth in Hallowe'en disguise. Who has not craved to rip the mask of myth off truth's face?*
>
> *The Freedmenmen believe that the physical universe was created after a complex series of couplings among the lesser deities, both male and female. This occurred during a drunken office party, held in Heaven by God, celebrating the successful creation of air. All men may read of such matters in the sacred writings, notably the Orange County Bible, the* Talmud Te Ching, *and the* Torah' Ra Buum Di-'ey.
>
> **—from "Coming of Age on Arruckus," by the Princess Serutan**

The man staggered forward a few steps, fell heavily onto the ground. He was a speck, landscape-dwarfed, out-shouted by the silent, uncaring Arruckusian sun. Sugar swished beneath him as he struggled to raise himself up. His shirt, tattered in shreds hanging loose-limp on his ravaged frame, yet could be read on its front-stencilled motto: "My forebears folded space to Arruckus, and all I souvenired was this lousy sweat-shirt."

Beneath the sweatshirtrags another garment could be seen: a purple napkin, open upon the chest, its tie-strings knotted around the neck like an apron, Freedmenmen-style.

The man's eyes, dulled in their red-on-red, grew glassy.

Squinting into the glare of the sun, he shielded his gaze with a hand and focussed on a dot circling in the pale Arruckus sky. *Just as I thought,* he thought. *A maltose falcon. What the Freedmenmen call the "sweet bird of youth."*

Then he thought: *It senses death.*

Two men had brought him here the day previous, on the command of Baron Vladimir Hardchargin. They had left him to die. The pretzels would claim him, destroy all evidence of his death. The Emperor would issue a token protest, call a pro forma commission to investigate. After all, he was still Imperial Plane-tologiste. The forms must be obeyed, lest that precise system of social and political order, the *nofreelunches,* be imperilled.

They'll do anything to keep Arruckus quiet, he thought. *Anything for the beer.* Then he thought: *Come to think of it, I could use a brew myself.*

He smiled. All the forces of the Imperium—the

83

Emperor, the Schlepping Guild, the Boni Maroni, the Great Big Houses, NOAMCHOMSKI—all walked carefully where the beer was concerned. Yet they spoke of the pretzels of Arruckus as mere inconveniences or oddities, and dismissed the Freedmenmen as a quaint tribe of savages.

Yet I know the truth, he thought. *The pretzels create the beer!*

"It's simple ecology," he said aloud. "The pretzels, roaming beneath the topsugars of the planet, come into contact with the subsurface salts. For a time they bear the giant white macro-crystals on their shiny baked skins, like barnacles. The saltrocks act as an irritant, transforming the normally timid pretzel into a rampaging monster."

He paused, racked with grief, thought: *Most people don't understand that the pretzel is really a very docile creature!*

He gasped, struggled to collect himself, went on. "These ferocious salt-bearing pretzels are the 'Three-Ringed Yokes of Madness' cited in Freedmenmen song and legend.

"But eventually the salt triggers a process of snacko-catalysis, and the pretzels break down into salted peanuts. These are used by the Freedmenmen for their religious rituals. Underground pockets of these peanuts are metabolized by native yeasts. Rainwater filters down and is trapped in these pockets, combining with the yeast-peanut mixture to form 'brew.' This ferments in deep pools, maturing in time into beer."

He stumbled forward, fell, got up, staggered a few

steps, fell, lay there, thought: *This was first discovered by the early Freedmenmen settlers of the planet some four hundred years (Standard) ago.* They had fled here in an effort to escape religious persecution, he remembered.

"Other peanuts, left on the planet's surface during its dry season, become dehydrated, and develop into the proto-pretzel, plant-animal-snack hybrid called 'nuggets,'" he continued. "When the rainy season returns, the water leaches all salt out of the nuggets. They bake in the sun, acquiring the characteristic shiny brown coloring. This triggers their final growth stages: first into 'baby sticks,' then into 'giant sticks,' until finally they develop into fully-adult pretzels. They burrow underground and begin to roam for food, and the cycle continues."

He stood unsteadily, his own thoughts a welter of shout-thinking in his own mind.

None of them know this! Only I—and the Freedmenmen!

He knew something else. His nose detected the tang of ripe yeasts and brewscents of pungent, sweet esters —nasal data, irrefutable and sufficient, of a pre-beer brewpool hundreds of feet below the surface on which he now stood, lurched, fell. The beer was nearing its maturation point. Soon thousands of gallons of it would erupt in a single massive "beer blast," exploding onto the surface of the planet, to collect in the small pockets the Freedmenmen called "bellies."

He had to leave that area! As quickly as possible! And in an orderly manner!

Standing, he set off, a feeble-paced thing. He had

85

been on-sugar like this before, without Freedkit or 'thopter, beermug or filtcig. But on those occasions he had managed to send up a signal to a Freedmenmen patrol, or at worst summon Schmai-gunug himself, and ride to a hootch, to safety.

Now he had nothing—neither ferndoc nor caltrans, link-ray nor flamtap. And he knew he was hundreds of kilometers from the aid of anyone, from the people of graben or pan, of bled or sink, of erg or eek or aargh. Let alone his good friends, the Freedmen-men.

Here's to good friends, he thought, and stumbled again.

Somewhere a voice in the back of his mind screamed that he was thirsty, that he needed water or beer, and food. Another voice in the side of his mind screamed back that he knew, he knew, and to please shut up. Then a third voice in the front of his mind screamed how could anybody get any thinking done with those two voices in his mind screaming at each other like that.

The falcon circled down lower to inspect the figure crawling across the sugar.

A thought took shape in the man's fatigue-addled brain: perhaps if he lightened his load, he might travel faster.

He tore off the sweatshirt remnants and tossed them aside, watching them flutter deadly onto the crystal-flecked ground. He now wore only the loose trousers, and the purple napkin, the *bib*, given him when he had been accepted by the Freedmenmen years after his arrival on this planet.

86

He stopped and looked dazedly at the cloth. He considered jettisoning it, too, but stayed his hand as it triggered a memory of the ceremony in which they'd presented him it.

They'd all assembled in Hootch Grabr. Spilgard'd been there, and the Shutout Mopes. All'd stood silent in the great dark stone cavern as he'd knelt, and the nabe'd repeated the traditional formula in the ancient Varietese.

"Keynes," Spilgard'd said. "Indie prod house seeks helmer, scribe for aussie bio pic."

He'd replied, not knowing what it meant but having studied it phonetically, "Cable kid-vid tallies down; prexy scores distribber woes."

"Webs in black on o-and-o's."

"B'cast pundits nix A.M. stereo."

Spilgard had then turned to the tribe and said, "Prod o'runs boost Universal sci-fi epic tab."

As one they had replied, "Need max U.S., o'seas b.o., plus solid homevid followup, for Xmas gala desert saga."

Then Spilgard had turned to him and'd said, "Rise, Keynes. Now you are of our tribe. You are Freedmenmen. Our meat is yours. Your meat is ours." The nabe'd placed around his neck the purple napkin. "This bib's for you."

The maltose falcon landed a few feet from the recumbent human figure. Keynes was unaware of it, his mind absorbed in the memory of his acceptance by the people who truly owned—no; managed—this planet, and its pretzels, and its beer.

A rumble began deep within the ground, and the bird took off in a flap of panic. The last thought Keynes was aware of, before the ground rose up in a massive eruption of suds and sugar, was an appreciation of irony: that the brew he so craved to quench his more-than-one-beer thirst, would be the agent of his death.

My father, the Pahdedbrah Emperor, said once of Baron Vladimir Hardchargin, "Inside every fat man there is a thin man signalling wildly to get out and eat everything in sight. That's why the man is fat in the first place."

—from "Daddy Dearest: Memoirs of an Imperial Girlhood," by the Princess Serutan

"They are surely dead, m'Lord Baron," said the guard. "Keynes, the Lady Jazzica, the boy Pall—all have been taken out into the sugars, and all—"

"Ah ah!" the Baron said suddenly, holding up a plump hand of admonition. "Don't tell me. I don't want to know."

"Of course, Sire." The guard bowed and withdrew.

The Baron turned to Peter De Vries. Save for a retinue of attendants, the two were alone in the vast Main Hall of the Governor's Palace in Arrucksack. "Can you believe the fool, Peter?" the fat man snorted. "Why, he would have told me everything—where they were taken, how they died, what did they know, when did they know it—"

88

"A rash and thoughtless thing, my Lord Baron," De Vries replied absently.

"Thoughtless? Treacherous, man!" The Baron reached out a flabby arm and grasped a handful of melon balls, gobbled them lasciviously, spat the seeds into his pudgy hand, flung them into an aide's face. "What if our illustrious Emperor, Shaddap IV, convenes a Juris Rancho Grande to investigate Keynes's disappearance? As a matter of course I shall be summoned to testify."

"And you wish deniability, my Lord."

"Of a certainty. What I don't know, or what I say I don't know—or, at least, what it cannot be proven I *do* know, cannot hurt me. Depend on it, Peter: men in power are innocent until not indicted, not brought to trial, and not proven guilty."

The Baron gestured to an aide. The young man approached, bowed low. "That guard who was just here," the Baron said. "See that he is dismissed. No severance pay. Nothing."

The aide bowed and left. The Baron, smacking his lips and drying his hands, produced from a large portfolio a sheaf of drawings, all done of samflax pastelles on extralong zigzagpaper.

"Come, Peter," he said with relish. "Take a look at these sketches. This is for the cloak room. A knockout, eh?"

De Vries scanned the picture, pursed his lips. "Quite handsome, Baron."

The Baron dropped his hands limply, looked up with a pout. "You don't like it."

"Well, Sire, interiors are not Jonzun Fillup's strong suit—"

"Jonzun Fillup did not do these sketches. I did."

De Vries examined the drawings again. "They do show a certain raw exuberance of line, my Lord."

The Baron frowned, paused. "Is that good, Peter?"

"For a cloak room, yes, it's most appropriate."

The Baron smiled, apparently content. He rolled up the cloak room drawing and unfurled another. "This is the lobby to the main theatre. Notice how I've co-ordinated the carpets and the drapes with the hat-check girls' sarongs."

"Most appealing, Sire."

The Baron looked at De Vries, said coyly, "You know, Jonzun Fillup said he thought my designs were amazingly good for an amateur."

"I'm sure he did, Sire."

The Baron scowled. "Don't patronize me, Peter. I know your opinion of Jonzun Fillup. But look at his headquarters planet for Antares Teleport and Tele-path. The Ionic entablature covering the north pole? Genius!"

"It's not to my taste, Baron," the Mantan said. "But I grant you, his legitimacy makes him the perfect architect for your purposes. And you're just the sort of client he likes."

The Baron laughed and slapped his gelatinously-quivering belly. "We're going to take this miserable planet, re-design it from top to bottom, and convert it into the most elegant cocktail lounge in the known

90

universe. And we shall begin by capturing those damned pretzels."

De Vries frowned, said, "That's an ambitious plan, Baron. They're big."

"Yes, yes, they're immense, certainly," the Baron said impatiently. "But just think how superbly they'll go with the house beer. Besides, we cannot simply let them roam free. It's out of the question. One can't expect the cream of Imperial society to frequent a club where, at any moment, a wall may be smashed in by a marauding giant pretzel."

"Assuredly not, Sire."

The Baron nodded. "First we shall capture the pretzels. And then, I do believe we must exterminate the Freedmenmen. A savage and untrustworthy people, Peter. I think I shall leave that job for Filp-Rotha. Yes, I shall. He thinks to merely step in and rule here when I assume my directorship of NOAMCHOMSKI. Let dear Filp earn his piece of this deliciously rich Arruckusian pie. After all, Peter, a little bit of genocide never hurt anybody."

Besides, the Baron thought, *he'll enjoy it. Filp will take great pleasure in wiping out the Freedmenmen. Unless he'll wish to dragoon them into service as busboys . . . ?*

No, they're too damned mystical, with their prattle of messiahs and their skulking about in those odd suits. They must go.

The Baron rang for food, then thought contemptuously: *If there's one thing I cannot abide, it's a mystical busboy.*

91

Mauve'Bib said: "Show me your civilization's most precious values, and I'll show you mine. Go on, show me. Please. Just a peek. Just one precious value. All right, be that way. Don't show me."

—from "A Time for Pompous Titles: Memories of Mauve'Bib," by the Princess Serutan

"Get their entrees, Spilgard, and let's move it," said the voice.

The apparent leader of the troop, standing in shadow before Jazzica, turned to address the speaker. "Let's move what, Janis?"

The other man grumbled, then said, "It. It's an expression—'let's move it.' I don't know. It. You know."

"I command here," said the leader sternly. "And I shall decide when it is to be moved, and what it is."

Spilgard! Jazzica thought. *The nabe I met back in Arrucksack.*

Spilgard stepped toward her into the light. From his vantage point six inches away, Pall tensed, right hand relaxed and ready to whiplashsnap for his wallet.

"I know you, woman," the nabe said. His eyes, depthless red-on-red, narrowed as he examined Jazzica. "We have met."

"At the Governor's Palace at Arrucksack," she replied. "There did Spilgard and I join meat."

Spilgard turned to examine Pall. "And this is your bunky, your son," he said. "Word has spread among our volksritr, our people, that he is the Laserium al-Dilah', the Bright Light of the Italian Love Song. When such news first reached my gnocchis, my ears, I

92

was klauskinski—skeptical as to the veracity of a religious-based rumor. But much of the prophecy has already been lyfah-ryli, fulfilled (usually with reference to apocryphal or legendary assertions). Still, it would not do to declare the Mahi-mahi, the day of arrival of the messiah, prematurely. More engleberthumperdinck, proof, is needed."

"We waste time, Spil," called the one named Janis. "Do we obey the sacred injunction to assure foremost the strength of the tribe by taking their entrees, or what?"

"Let the boy-man and his mother-woman join my group," Spilgard announced. "Let them accompany us to hootch, that we might see if the lad is truly the Laserium al-Dilah'."

"They are meat-lean, two off-worlders," Janis snarled. "Like as mayhap not they spy for the Hardchargin devil, or work in the Guild's employ. Or perhaps they serve the Emperor—scouts for another cursed documentary about us for the Pahdedbrah Broadcasting System." He said mimickingly, " 'They are a simple people, yet with a rich cultural heritage all their own.' Pah!" He spat in disgust.

"We serve neither Hardchargin nor PBS," Pall said forcefully. "Who claims we do, lies."

"Easy, my young wally," Spilgard soothed. Turning to Janis, he said with an edge, "Do you challenge my rule in this matter?"

"Spilgard has been known to make mistakes," Janis said, stubborn.

I could silence this Janis by telling him to get out of the kitchen, Jazzica thought.

93

But before she could speak, Spilgard roared, "I tell you, Janis, they have my countenance!"

An agitated murmur arose from the crowd. Pall heard one man ask another, "They have his countenance—does that mean they have his face?"

Hearing this, another cried, "Spilgard gives them his face! He gives meat to the off-worlders!"

"He gives them the meat of his face!"

"No, no!" called the nabe. "It means . . ."

But the air was rent by a gabble of cheering, making futile further reply.

A-h-h-h-h-h-h-h-h, they are an excitable people, thought Jazzica. *A people who could be whipped into a frenzy at the drop of a hat. How useful that could be to us. A-h-h-h-h-h-h-h-h-h.*

"Come," Spilgard said. "We must return to Hootch Grabr."

They fell into marching order, their sweatsuit hoods up and covering their heads. Pall marked with what stealth and precision they moved. As he took his place in procession, he noticed a figure beside him. It was a girl-child, with elfin face and a generous mouth.

"You must not lose step," the girl said. Her voice was laughfilled with liltsong, her newspeak bigmouth smile-faced with happytalk.

"You look . . . familiar . . ." Pall said. "Haven't we . . . met?"

"I am Loni, daughter of Bob," she said.

"I am Pall, son of Duke Lotto Agamemnides."

Shyly, dimpling a smile, she said, "You have not the eye of the Egad."

He looked puzzled, then noticed she was pointing to

his own brown eyes, their whites normal and clear. Her eyes were the typical red-on-red of her people.

Even their girls-children drink the beer, Pall thought. *It is a France-like thing.*

They marched for several hours until they came to a series of caves walled 'round by rock-candy hazy white and opaque in the waning sunlight. Spilgard assigned sentries to keep watch as they made camp. Many Freedmenmen removed their sweatshirts, revealing a variety of plain shirts and blouses underneath. Worn on each, tied around the neck, was a purple napkin.

Jazzica watched in awe as the Freedmenmen silently went about their efficient routines, mounting westinglobes for light, preparing cookfires for carmelbrew, distributing mugs of a frothing golden liquid. *Beer,* she thought. *This will be our first true exposure to it. I hope Pall knows of the risks, and that he will drink it responsibly and in moderation.* She felt an abrupt fear, shuddered. *Surely he will not be so foolish as to try to operate any heavy machinery . . .*

She looked up as Spilgard approached. "Your young wally and our beaver have made linkage," he said, gesturing.

Jazzica looked, saw that, across an open space, against a wall, Pall sat with the girl-child Loni, deep in conversation. The implications disturbed her.

I must warn Pall about time-making with that girl-child, Jazzica thought. *We must win the respect of these people, yes—but to hire them, not join them. It would prove fatal to our purpose were Pall to any of their women lovemake to!*

And possibly upknock!

95

Pall saw his mother regarding him from the distance. *She plays a dangerous game,* he thought.

Then he smiled at Loni. She said, "Here, drink this," and handed him a small beermug in which a cool golden liquid foamed. She held up her own mug. "Let us elbow-bend the cold 'n' frosty," she murmured. "Steak for dinner sometime soon."

He nodded and sipped.

The taste was sharp to his tongue. Waftings of yeastscent made his nose flicker with their bite. Concealed in the liquid was a profusion of evanescent pinpricks, and these seemed to explode in an abrasive fusillade as he swallowed, grating down his throat. His body felt injected with air. An afterdreg of sudsfoam remained on his upper lip; Loni laughed and wiped it off with the purple napkin she wore around her neck.

"You like?" she said.

"Hell, yes," he replied.

Suddenly a thing within him reared up, sought escape. In an abrupt burst it flew out of his mouth, invisible but rending the air with a sharp, guttural bark.

"What have you done to me!" Pall raged. "There're demons in my stomach!"

Loni stared, laughed.

"Oh, Pall Agamemnides, that's just beerburp," she gasped with mirth. "The breath of Schmai-gunug gathers in the brew. We release it when we drink. Thus do we free it to be breathed again, that Schmai-gunug may live and the tribe prosper."

A male voice nearby said, "It's basic ecology, Pall Agamemnides."

96

"Let's have another one," Loni said.

She removed from her pack a canister, and applied to its top a swysknife, using one of its attachments to puncture the top. Then she solemnly poured the liquid into the beermug, down its center. A roiling white head rose up from the bottom of the mug, concealing most of the golden clarity.

"Now we must wait for foamfall," she said, watching the cloud of bubbles slowly disperse. "Not before then may we drink."

Pall suddenly said, "Try this."

Taking the canister from her, he poured its remnants into another beermug, this time tilting the vessel and letting the beerflow land halfway up its side. The beer collected placidly in the mug, rising to fullness without a head of white froth.

Loni stared, amazed.

"You pour without foam!" she whispered. "Your head is small!"

"Just an idea I had—" he began.

But she had risen and held up his mug for all to see. "Behold!" she cried. "Pall Agamemnides pours without foam!"

All activity ceased. From all over the camp Freedmenmen stopped and looked at the girl, at the mug in her held-aloft hand, at the beer and its headless top.

" 'And he shall be wise, yet he shall have no head,' " someone quoted softly.

"He is the Laserium al-Dilah'!" Loni cried joyfully.

Pall was aware of all eyes on him, of expressions of awe and wonder in those eyes.

Have a caution, he thought. *My status as holy man could at this juncture gain significant reinforcement—or suffer direst setback. This's a crucial possibility-nexus.*

"Behold the beer without head," Pall intoned. "I pour it into my own head." He held up high the mug, drank deep. Then he held up the drained vessel. "Thus does the . . . the head of . . ." He paused, allowed for beerburp, continued, "My head . . . I am the head! Of the beer!" He nodded. *Got it.* "I am the Beer Head of Doon!"

The Freedmenmen broke into cheers, upholding their own mugs and drinking in salute.

Yet Pall heard it indistinctly, for the narcotic effects of the beer had begun to work on him. A vaporous plume rose from his stomach into his head. He felt a pleasing lightness, as though his brain were newly-supported by a gossamer cloud of well-being. He felt lulled, expansive.

Then the full force of the drug took hold of him, as his normal balance of emotion-states suddenly tipped wildly. Now, rather than experiencing a positive reaction of feelgood uplift in response to external events, he felt himself generating his own exhilaration-response. Veils of social conditioning and learned-restraint patterns were ripped away. Revealed now were raw, explosive sources of self-generated life-pleasure, good-mood, and wanting-to-go-berserk.

"Hey," he said, extending a limp hand in loose pawflop to the girl-child Loni. "You're pretty."

Yet there was a distant calculating part of him that

noted with detachment the effects of the beer, feeding into merciless mental computation the cold data of numerous possible futures. He slumped against the rock-candy wall and leaned back, his field of vision taking in a section of the cave in which people now saluted each other and downed foaming beermugs of the golden drink.

This, he realized, was the Freedmenmen path. The Golden Path of Beer!

And his inner vision at that moment glimpsed a series of possible futures. Many of them reached only part-way into the future, depicting a variety of possible-series-of-events that might unfold over the next thirty seconds.

In each, he saw himself approaching the girl-child Loni and requesting another mugful. The variations were manifold: in some he walked, in others crawled, in still others sort of slid-lurched.

But beyond these lay one particular vision—indeed, was the focal point of all the disparate crawlings-forward and beer-swillings, the one toward which they all tended, seemed to lead inexorably.

And he knew it was the one possible future he must avoid.

It was a vision of himself, drinking vaster and vaster draughts of the brew until, half mad, he leaped up in drunken beerfrenzy, attempting to sing "Girl-Childs Just Want to Have Fun-Pleasure" in harmony with himself, and began taking off his clothes and dancing about, until finally upthrowing and out-passing, cold.

My father, the Pahdedbrah Emperor, spent much time—both while conducting the necessary official business of the Imperium and, after, among us, in familial repose—wearing a dress. Did this impair his effectiveness as a ruler? History has already answered. Who asked you, History? we might respond.

—from "In My Father's House, in His Room, and Especially Rummaging Around in His Junk Drawer," by the Princess Serutan

Pall shook his head to clear it, looked up with fuzzy, if trained, awareness. Barely more than a few minutes had passed since his experience of possible-futures. He was still seated on the ground, his back against a wall of rock candy. Nearby was the girl-child, Loni. He began to speak to her, then noticed that she was looking beyond him, frowning. He followed her gaze, and saw the man called Janis in dispute with Spilgard.

And Janis was gesturing . . . toward him!

"He is a documentarist," Janis said vehemently. "How else explain his skill with the brew, save for his prior experience invading other peoples and cultures?"

"The signs say he is the Laserium al-Dilah'," Spilgard said. "And his skill is a gift from God."

"He will have camera crews and soundmen here within a week!"

"Be silent, Janis."

Janis leaped back and pointed at Pall. "Then I invoke the amway rule!" he cried. "Let us meet in rankout and see which shall prevail!"

Jazzica stepped forward. Pitching her voice to its most irritatingly nasal she began, "Get *out* of the—"

100

Spilgard held up a hand. "You must be silent, woman," he said. "Janis has challenged your bunky. He has invoked the amway rule, as is his right. Now your son must provide Janis with satisfaction. Or, he may find a congenial group of friends, neighbors, and relatives willing to buy the rights to a franchise entitling *them* to provide Janis with satisfaction. Your son must respond, or be banished."

"No problem," Pall called out, rising unsteadily. "C'mon, Janis, le's go."

"Your mind is beer-potchkied, Pall Agamemnides," Loni whispered. "You cannot face Janis in such a state."

"Why may not I cannot do what any man could maybe . . . uh . . ." Pall waved off the girl, impatient with words and unable to speak now in any but the most simple declarative sentences. "Janis. You. Come."

They approached each other as the Freedmenmen moved back against the cave walls, creating a ring around a clear fighting floor. Pall could sense, amid beerfume mindhaze, that all his awareness training and insult drilling had prepared him for just such an encounter. To the extent that he was able to focus them, he kept his eyes on Janis's, saw the red-on-red of beer addiction, and an additional red of hate.

He's angry, Pall thought. *That's an advantage for me. I'll let him make the first move.* He remembered what Loni had whispered to him just prior to taking his stance.

He will attack your mother, she had said. *This we*

101

*have seen him do many times. And beware his ability to
reverse, and send your barb back against you. He is fast,
if not subtle.*

"Off-worlder," Janis said with contempt. "Your
mother is like a pack of gum—five sticks for a nickel."

It was as she had predicted. Pall replied, softly, "At
least I have a mother, Janis."

His opponent smiled, but something in his eyes
betrayed surprise.

A murmur passed among the assembled Freedmenmen. "The boy fights well," one whispered.

Janis said in a sudden rush, "If brains were birds,
your head'd be an empty sky."

Pall thought, said: "If good sense, sound judgment,
and measured temperament were a cat, you'd be a
dog."

"Then I'd bite you!" Janis snarled.

A gasp issued forth from the onlookers. Pall reeled.
That was close! he thought.

Jazzica thought, *Pall has never ranked-out a man like
this before! Is he . . . capable of prevailing?*

A tension had filled the air. All seemed to sense that
the next sally would prove decisive. Janis eyed Pall,
sneered, "Only a woman drinks beer without a head."
He turned to the crowd, in evident expectation of
triumph.

Pall looked downcast, as though Janis's comment had
sunk home and found its mark. It was a feint taught him
by Drunken Omaha. *Let him think he's got you,* the
tutor had counseled. *Then open up a mouth.*

"Better to be a woman, drinking beer without a
head—" Pall said, his deep training prompting him to

102

pause a vital split-second before concluding, "—than to be a man without a head, drinking beer without a woman."

There came a moment, a split-instant, of infinite silence. Pall stood aside as the larger man drained his face of color, looked like a dead thing.

"I . . ." Janis began.

But there was no more to be said, no remark that could best the double-flipping retort Pall had sent cutting into the sugar-fat flesh of the man's self-esteem. Janis turned away and, wordlessly, walked off in a slump of defeat.

Pall started to go after him—and felt a firm hand on his arm. He looked up into the grim face of Spilgard.

"Follow not, lad," he said. "Janis will do what all Freedmenmen must do, upon rankout defeat. He'll wander off into the sugars and give his meat to Schmai-gunug."

"But . . . why?" Pall asked. "He's alive, and well, and—"

"And in disgrace, and sulking," Spilgard growled. "A man thus self-pitying seeks solace, and will find it in food. He'd eat beyond his share of our meagre store of entrees—"

"—and bring ruin to the tribe," Pall said, nodding. "I understand." He paused, then said, "But here is a thing: you make reference to 'the meat of the body.' If meat be so rare on Arruckus, well . . ." Pall groped for words. ". . . why not, when someone dies, or is sent out into the wilds . . . why not take his body, and . . . you know . . . meat is meat . . ."

Spilgard looked at him amazed. "Are you suggesting

103

that we make meat of our people?" he asked. "That we eat their remains?"

"The meat of the body belongs to the tribe, say," Pall shrugged, blushing red. "Anyway, just a thought."

"You outgross me," the nabe said, shaking his head. "Your rankout is excellent. But this eating of the meat of others is a disgusting thing, Pall Agamemnides."

"Needs a better name'n that, Spil," one man called. "Like to make a man's tongue strangle itself to speak it."

"Aye," muttered many of the troop.

"True," Spilgard said firmly. To Pall he said, "We remember when you cried treachery upon first beer-burp, claiming you'd swallowed a demon. Therefore let you be called Assol, which is the word we employ for men who act thuswise ridiculous. That shall be your secret name among us."

"Assol," Pall mused, measuring the sound and sense of it. "It's not the greatest name in the known universe, is it . . . ?"

"It be only your secret name," Spilgard said with a trace of noticeable irritation. "Now you'll be wanting an official Freedmenmen name, which all may call you to the meat of your face."

Pall thought a moment, then spied Loni in the crowd. The moonlight glowed cool silver on the purple napkin around her neck, and he recalled with an inward-warming-up-feeling how she had cleansed his lip of sudsfoam. "What do you call these napkins?" he asked, pointing to those worn by all the tribe.

Spilgard looked puzzled, indicated his own. "Why, Pall who is Assol, it is the color mauve, and it is a bib.

104

We call this a mauve bib." He looked at the others, shrugging.

"That shall be my name, then," Pall said. "That, plus my given name, lest I forget my father, and be similarly forgotten by his executors. From this day I shall be Mauve'Bib Agamemnides!"

He shot a glance around the gathered tribe in triumph, yet saw averted eyes, strained smiles hiding embarrassment, heard suppressed titter-laughs.

A voice emerged from the rear of the group. "Pretty stupid name, Spil . . ."

The nabe stepped forward. "Enough," he said. "Be you called Pall Mauve'Bib, and there be an end to't."

"Yet I am also Duke Pall Agamemnides, if my father be truly fired," Pall said with a sudden non-boyish sobriety.

"We understand," Spilgard said.

"And I'm also the Laserium al-Dilah'."

"Yes, yes, we remember."

"I also may be the Kumkwat Haagendasz, don't forget."

Spilgard turned to the troop, said, "Who is Secretary of the Recording this week? Raita? Write these down on the Pad of Memos, lest we forget this endless, prodigious flood of names, titles—"

Another voice hissed, "Pall!"

It was the Lady Jazzica, who looked on with a feeling of abrupt fear. *He must not alienate them with all those names,* she thought.

Pall joined her off to one side, said with edgy wariness, "Yes, Mother?"

"These are a proud people," Jazzica said softly.

"They are bound together by strong cultural and social ties."

Pall's eyes widened in horror. "Then it's true!" he cried-whispered.

"What's true . . . ?"

"You *are* a documentarist for PBS!"

She shook her head impatiently. "No," she hissed. "Now listen to me. We can make use of these people to regain control of Arruckus from Baron Hardchargin. Do you understand? The Freedmenmen can help put us back in business!" She permitted herself to glare at him with eyes blazing rage. "But not if you scare them off with all those titles!"

Pall's face went blank. He looked at his mother with the pan of a dead thing. "No," he said. "There is something for us here beyond all that, Mother. Something larger than the family business. It is a really big thing I am talking." Pall's eyes gleamed bright in the dimness as he whispered, "Religion!"

"Mauve'Bib!" called the gathered Freedmenmen. "Mauve'Bib!"

"My people want me, Mother," Pall said, and turned on his heel to rejoin Spilgard and the troop.

And they gathered around Pall Mauve'Bib, the offworlder called Assol, the Laserium al-Dilah', or whoever he was. Hands pressed his, accompanied by the ritual murmurings.

"I join meat with Pall Mauve'Bib."

"Your meat is ours. Our meat is yours."

"Nice to meat you, Pall Mauve'Bib."

And the Lady Jazzica, looking on, had thoughts in her mind.

Now what will happen?

We must take care that we do not ascribe undue importance to chance in the affairs of men. Just as the human mind is a kind of cause-and-effect generator, so is the indeterminacy of action and reaction a concomitant force tending away from predictibility. Hence the ramifications, the fundamental, because consciousness is similar like a big box, so you've got, say, an animal in this box. Who wants another beer?

—from "Mauve'Bib: The Incoherent Ramblings,"
compiled by the Princess Serutan

On the occasion of his sixteenth birthday, Filp-Rotha mortally insulted his one-hundredth gladiator. The event, held in the mammoth Gladome, was attended by the entire population of the planet Getty Premium, homeworld of House Hardchargin. Also present were sundry representatives of the Great Big Houses and the Imperium.

Presiding over the meet was the Baron himself, returned from his administrative and interior decorative duties on Arruckus. He observed the contest from his luxury loge box, along with Peter De Vries, the Mantan.

"Observe, Peter," the Baron purred, gesturing toward the arena floor, where Filp-Rotha had just appeared. "The crowd is eager for combat. When Filp wins, as he undoubtedly shall, they will hail him as hero."

De Vries watched as the youth, clad in the traditional white linen slacks and sport shirt, deconstructed jacket and neck medallion, performed the customary dedicatory exercises—waving to the crowd, offering casual shrugs, miming chip shots with a 9-iron. Effortlessness was the key to a good performance, De Vries knew. He acknowledged with grudging reluctance that the shanana-Baron handled himself well.

"The boy has style," he said quietly, as Filp-Rotha assumed his combat position. "Of course, considering that his opponents are invariably drugged, hypnotized, and deprived of sleep for a week . . ."

"You are a purist, Peter," the Baron said. "But come, tell me what the Emperor's envoy said."

The Mantan sighed. The Baron was not paying full attention; the ensuing dialogue would be frustrating. "His Fantastic Imperialosity has expressed impatience with . . . progress on Arruckus," he said carefully. "The Emperor desires to know why so little seems to have been done in the way of capturing and domesticating the pretzels. The plan, he reminds you, was to make of them a freebie thing, for the Happy Hour."

The Baron snorted, jowls quivering. "His Grandiositousness knows full well how difficult it is to capture the beasts, Peter. Surely you pointed out that they rove the deepest sugars, where our patrols have difficulty going."

"Naturally, Baron," De Vries said. "I also—"

"Oh, look, they've begun."

The Mantan glanced down onto the field. Filp-Rotha had taken his place upon the slightly-raised platform, in a swivelling upholstered armchair behind a desk. On the desk stood a microphone. To his right, on ground level, was another chair—fixed, without arms, and canted at an angle acknowledging the desk but mainly open to the full view of the audience.

A ranker, in the customary dark suit, white shirt, and tie, had emerged from the doors under the stands and was walking toward this second chair. The crowd—some four and half billion—gave token cheer. Filp-Rotha stood at the desk, applauding the approach of his opponent.

"Isn't he a lovely boy," the Baron said. "Peter, tell me—am I sufficiently depraved to have carnal relations with my own nephew?"

De Vries had to think a moment on the thing. "Not usually, my Lord."

"Oh, pooh," the Baron said. "Anyway, continue."

"The Emperor wishes to know why the construction and decoration of the main lounge rooms is taking so long."

"Why, we're working with all possible speed!" the Baron protested. "Jonzun Fillup and I meet every day—and I'll tell you something, Peter. I actually think I'm having an influence on him. He told me as much yesterday. 'You and your red velvet banquettes, Baron —you're beginning to seduce me with them.' Oh, the man is a charmer!"

De Vries sighed and tried to concentrate on the bout. On the field below, Filp-Rotha had just deflected his opponent's comment about his shirt. The shanana-Baron then countered with a complicated jibe involving the ranker's face, the weather, and certain notorious sexual practices on the planet Delta-Pavlova of a species of sentient moss. The crowd roared.

"The Emperor makes a suggestion, my Lord," De Vries said gloomily.

"Now—oh, listen to that, Peter. Filp just called the man a bar of soap. How clever. And what is it His Praiseworthiness suggests?"

"That you double your work schedule by impressing into service a squadron of Freedmenmen."

The Baron turned and stared at De Vries in alarm. His voice was a croaking thing. "He does?" he husked.

"His Majesty wants the Shadvlad opened quickly and quietly, lest word leak out that his Hardehaurhar were involved in its . . . acquisition. After all, m'Lord . . ." De Vries said with delicacy. "He is Emperor, yes—but even he knows that the Great Big Houses will not sit still for unilateral displays of terrorist-bouncing."

"But . . . the Freedmenmen . . . they're worse than useless," the Baron protested. "And there are so few of them! It's hardly worth the effort to hunt them down. Besides . . ." He gave a little smile, chubbychin facefat wreathed with seams. "I'm extremely busy. Jonzun Fillup says he needs my fabric motifs for the Ladies and Female Life Forms Lounge next week."

"He knows many professional designers, my Lord. Couldn't he—"

De Vries regretted the thought before it was ever completed. The Baron whirled and shot a sharp glance at him. "He says he prefers my ideas!" he snapped. "Or do you think he merely flatters?"

"I simply report what the Emperor's man told me," the Mantan said with quiet dignity.

110

He turned to the arena, in time to witness the ranker stand and, livid with rage, shout that Filp-Rotha resembled a slug. The crowd gasped; such overtly angry deportment was almost unheard of. Filp-Rotha's opponents were invariably somehow handicapped for such contests, and usually submitted docilely after a few opening exchanges.

"Besides," the Baron continued. "His Majesty need fear nothing. The witnesses are gone: Duke Lotto deposed and on the skid row planet Boweron; the boy and his Boni Maroni mother surely dead in the sugars; the false accountant, Oyeah, doing standup for the prisoners on Salacia Simplicissimus."

"The Emperor wonders about the boy and his mother."

"But . . . they were seen wandering out into the wilds. No one can survive such a fate!"

"The envoy suggests they may have been rescued by Freedmenmen."

"Again with the Freedmenmen!" the Baron cried, red with anger. "If the Emperor wants the Freedmenmen rooted out and interrogated, let him do it! I have to talk to my wall upholsterers!"

On the field, Filp-Rotha had remained seated when his opponent had stood. He now rose to his feet and spoke several slashing lines in which the word "breath" was prominently featured.

The ranker staggered as the crowd exploded. Filp-Rotha flung both arms aloft in triumph.

"All right, Peter," the Baron said, abruptly weary. "Inform his Majesty's courier that I'll double the pretzel patrols and put the city construction workers on

111

overtime. I want the place completed as much as His Imperial Majestitude. Not for me, you understand," he murmured as, below, the crowd of four and half billion surged over the guard rails onto the field and lifted Filp-Rotha onto their shoulders. "I want it for Filp. For dear Filp. I do believe he's almost ready to assume control of Arruckus, Peter. When he does, I shall assume my position in NOAMCHOMSKI. And then . . ."

The Baron's eyes glowed primal greedy with piglust moneywant. "Then we shall discuss the possibilities inherent in casino gambling. Yes, we shall . . ."

The power of religion has been sorely underestimated by our scientists. No other force in history has been so effective at compelling human beings to say things in languages they don't understand.

—from Mauve'Bib's introduction to The New Improved Testament of the Orange County Bible, edited by the Princess Serutan

The Spilgard-led troop with its two sugarlost not-Freedmenmen refugees made hootchfall together, at last, in twilightime. Raw sugarrocks strewed the entrance to the basin of a cavernous surround.

Hootch Grabr!

Jazzica marvelled.

What had seemed from a distance to be rubble scattering the basin floor proved to be a well-camouflaged experimental garden. She recognized small plots of vegetables cultivating directly out of the

112

sugary soil. But there were other fenced-off areas of less familiar crops. They looked . . . strange. Jazzica's Boni Maroni training enabled her to tell, via nosesniff smellsense, that what was being agricultured were actually crude varieties of desert chicken pot pies, poverty veal parmigiana, and mutant Mexican-style shredded beefs in a zesty sauce.

Entrees! she thought. *They're actually growing entrees in the midst of this sugar. Could I have underestimated these people?*

She looked up, saw Spilgard watching her with suspicion.

"You see the mahn t'vahni, the food experiments," the nabe said.

"They are most impressive."

He shrugged. "Soybeans. Everything. Mashed, fried, tricked-up as best we can. It is an impossible thing, to grow true meat or vegetables in this sugary land." Then he turned upon her a stern eye. "Yet there are many who would pay much to know a little of such nothings."

Jazzica focussed on his words, listening *to* them and thinking *about* them. *I must respond,* she thought. *Yet what shall I . . . say?*

She turned to the nabe, said, "Would I betray the people whose life, saved by them, which even now enables me, in fact, to live, which I do, is mine own?"

Baffled, Spilgard frowned. "You have the weirdest way, woman," he said, shaking his head. "I'll not have to speak to you again, Schmai-gunug willing."

They were interrupted by a commotion at one of the cave entrances. A woman in hootch clothes was con-

113

fronting a small group of then-arriving Freedmenmen.
She had a generous mouth. Jazzica recognized a small
figure in their midst.

Pall!

Her son!

Her trained awareness confirmed the fact that the
boy, Pall, over there, to whom the woman was speaking, was her son. Yet she instantly permitted herself not
to experience anything.

The woman was pointing to Pall. "*This* outranked my
Janis?" she demanded. "This . . . boy-child?"

"He be more than that, Harrumf," Spilgard admon-
ished with newfound respect in his attitude.

"Man-child," she said grudgingly.

"More."

"Boy-man."

"Less."

"Baby-man. Man-boy. Boy-boy."

Pall stepped forward, and Jazzica heard the regret-
overtones and I'm-terribly-sorry harmonics in his
voice. "I—"

"Teen-boy. Youth-guy," the woman Harrumf said
with narrowed eyes. "Guy-man."

"You're close," Spilgard said. "Let'm be known as a
teen-man, and there be an end to't."

A murmur arose among the gathered troop, gradually condensing into a single discernible phrase: "Pall
Mauve'Bib-who-is-Assol is a teen-man!"

"And he," Harrumf said. "He outranked Janis?"

"I didn't want to," Pall said. "He . . . forced me to."

"Enough," Spilgard announced. "Assol, go with
Harrumf to your new quarters. From this day, for one

114

year, she is your branif—a woman whose man, found to be teetering on the brink of moral bankruptcy, you dismiss and replace. She shall restructure her life to accommodate your new management concepts."

He turned to Jazzica. "As for you, Jazzica—you are Boni Maroni. Mother of the Laserium al-Dilah', perhaps. And, though you bring no lamb chops, yet there are many among us who respect your powers. Therefore let you prepare for the Ceremony of Transfer. For our Revved-Up Mother is old, and soon goes to join Schmai-gunug, to roam forever erg and eek, through pot and pan, across the wide mizour-ri."

He addressed the girl-child who stood nearby. "Loni, prep Jazzica for the rite." He raised his voice to all the troop. "Let everyone else prepare to tap a keg."

As Loni took her arm and led her away, Jazzica's mind roiled with thought-about thoughts. *Ceremony of Transfer! Their Revved-Up Mother! By the beard of Claiborne's child! The Missionaria Phonibalonica has prepared these people well for us.*

Pall walked with Harrumf through a passageway into an intersecting network of caves. Westinglobes lined the walls, casting frostwhite see-where-you're-going light throughout the hootch.

"Walk this way, Assol," she said.

"If I could walk that way, Harrumf, I wouldn't need the corn oil," he replied.

"Starch. Corn starch," hissed the woman.

That's the second time I've gotten that wrong, he thought. *I must be more careful!*

They went on, past large cavernous chambers in which children could be seen in classroom situations,

115

and workshop areas in which men and women operated machinery for storing beer in bottles and canisters.

"Do most of the adults work in the beer shops, Harrumf?" Pall asked.

"The majority," she replied gruffly. "Some teach, some are full-time guards and scouts. Janis, he worked as a foamsman, he did. Likely you'll have his job."

Bet not on it, Pall thought.

His mouth opens
He says something—
Ah! Great!
I love it!
Ideas flow from his mind,
And his eyes! They explode! Look out!
Why do big hunks of wisdom appear
Whenever he is more or less near?
Just like me,
They long to be
An isthmus of total Selfhood!
Like . . . Him!
And his Mother, who is Beautiful.

> —from "Reflections: Poems of the Mauve'Bib
> Experience," by the Princess Serutan

Murmurings of crowd-gatherment filled the great cavernous hall as Jazzica was led out onto the ledge overlooking the floor. She estimated more than ten thousand Freedmenmen, with many more still amassing. The light in the hall was dim, gray featherings of twi-night doubleheaded crepuscularity.

"The Revved-Up Mother has been sent for," Spilgard, at her side, said. "Nutmen have been dispatched. Brewmasters are on call. Mug-wumps are on stand-by. All is in readiness."

I play a dangerous game, Jazzica thought.

Still more people were entering the cavern.

It was getting . . . crowded.

"In truth, I think it too early for this rite," Spilgard mused. "But it's the Revved-Up Mother. You know how cranky they can be. She's been calling through space and time for this all week."

"I will try to pass the test," Jazzica said.

She looked up and saw Pall enter, escorted by Harrumf and two small boys. They had generous mouths, and the beginnings of the eye of the Egad, the red-on-red of beer addiction.

So young! she thought. *They, too, play a dangerous game. And that broad-woman—their mother? She plays a dangerous game. Everywhere you look, somebody's playing a dangerous game. Yet if we are to bend these Freedmenmen to our will, and hire them as help for the business, we must play a dangerous game, too. Yet it is . . . dangerous.*

And it's no game!

A bustle commotioned at a far end of the hall. Jazzica looked, saw the crowd part. An old woman was carried on a litter through the throng to the steps leading up to the ledge. She was ancient, an old thing in a black robe, an aged woman of many years, whose elderliness was great in the magnitude of its dimension. Yet there sparkled in her eyes a youthful glittering, although the rest of her was still old.

Loni helped her stand down off the litter and escorted her up the steps. She stood before Jazzica and examined her.

"So you're the one," she husked. "The Shutout Mopes said you were the one who is the One."

"She was mistaken," Jazzica said. "I'm not the one who is the One. I'm the one who is the Other One."

"Close enough." She turned to Spilgard. "Tell them."

He nodded, faced the crowd, held up his hands until silence hushed throughout the chamber. "Two outfreekt strangers have come to us," the nabe announced. "One is the teen-man Assol-who-is-Pall Mauve'Bib. There are those who believe he is the Mahdl-T, the Laserium al-Dilah', the Messiah who will lead us against our enemies throughout the universe in an unstoppable jihad that will vanquish them for all time." He looked at Pall. "Great to have you with us tonight, Mauve'Bib."

Murmurous commentings arose in the cavern, crescendoing in a warm round of applause for Pall.

"Here too is his mother, Jazzica of the Weirdness," Spilgard continued. "To those who ask why I have named her thus, let them get themselves a load of this." He faced Jazzica, said, "The tribe awaits your greeting."

Jazzica smiled at the nabe, turned to address the crowd. "Spilgard honors that self which I, the boy's mother, have, or am."

Spilgard threw up his arms, called to the tribe, "Weirdness, right? Yet Revved-Up Mother Caramello has verified what the Shutout Mopes reported, that

118

Jazzica of the Weirdness shall become our next Revved-Up Mother, that we may not suffer the pain of withdrawal in our need of Revved-Up Motherings. Therefore, let the ceremony proceed."

Spilgard turned to two solemn men off to one side. "Nutmen, is there cocktail mix?"

"There is cocktail mix," said one of the pair. "But we have nothing to drink with it."

Spilgard addressed two other men. "Brewmasters, is there beer?"

"There is beer," said one of them. "But we have nothing to serve it in."

To a third pair of men the nabe said, "Mug-wumps, are there mugs?"

"There are mugs," came the ritual reply. "But we have nothing to nibble on."

"Let the cocktail mix be brought forward."

The two nutmen moved toward the front of the ledge, bearing between them a large metal bowl wrought with elaborate symbols and designs. In the bowl Jazzica saw a mound of small pebbles of various brownish hues. Her Boni Maroni trained nose detected salt, traces of sugardust, and an oddly familiar odor.

Mercy Bocuse! Jazzica thought with a shock. *That smells exactly like decomposed pretzels!*

"This is the cocktail mix," intoned Spilgard. "The nuts of Schmai-gunug—Remnant of His body, Seed of His Nuggets, Essence of Beer, Snack-Nibble of the Gods. Jazzica of the Weirdness—eat you then of these nuts."

One of the nutmen scooped a handful of the nuts out of the bowl and held it before Jazzica's face. The entire

119

cavern was silent. Jazzica carefully took a single small nut in her fingertips.

Salted peanuts, she thought. *Highly addictive. It will be virtually impossible to eat only one.*

Spilgard held up his hand to stay her momentarily.

He addressed the congregation.

"We have no meat, no fish."

As a single voice they replied, "Stix nix hix pix."

Spilgard said: "We have no vegetables, nor pasta."

"Stix nix hix pix."

The nabe said: "Because we have no entrees, therefore let us eat nuts."

In unison, the twenty thousand Freedmenmen replied, "Boffo."

"Nuts to me," Silgard said. "Jazzica of the Weirdness: nuts to you."

"Boffo," chanted the crowd.

He nodded to Jazzica.

Carefully, she placed the nut on her tongue. The congregation gave a collective intake of breath.

The nutman shoved the handful of nuts into her mouth.

There was a salty tang, and a presence of many slick rounded smoothnesses and flat-sheared little surfaces. Their woodenish hardness gave way to her grinding teeth in a collapsing, mealy crunch of nutpaste and in-her-mouth munchnoise. She masticated, feeling the nuts crumble into undifferentiated nutmass, making dry her mouth and lodging in her teeth. She swallowed, instantly felt an overwhelming craving for something to drink.

"Let us drink the beer of Schmai-gunug," Spilgard

proclaimed. "Brew of His death, and of the plains of Arruckus."

The brewmasters came forward with watertight bags of sloshing liquid, held one over a mug proffered by a mug-wump, and filled the vessel. The mug-wump handed it to Jazzica.

"Jazzica of the Weirdness: bend the elbow."

"Boffo," sighed the tribe.

Jazzica took the mug, sensing the beer's yeasty tang and seeing the ragged white foam-head subsiding. She took a mouth-filling gulp, and swallowed.

Smooth, she thought. *With a rich, full-bodied flavor.*

One of the brewmasters intoned with ritual solemnity, "How about a refill on that?"

"Boffo," replied the tribe.

Jazzica held out the mug, had it refilled, drank. An airy inflatedness began to accumulate inside her. And an eerie plume of spirit-haze seemed to rise from her stomach to her head. Unaccountably, she felt buoyant, giddy, unreasonably happy.

She held out the mug. "More," she commanded.

The brewmasters refilled the mug, and again she drank. "Jazzica of the Weirdness," Spilgard said, drama edging his voice. "Hold out your arms at fullest length, thus."

He showed her how, stretching out her arms to either side, making of her body a T-shape.

I know this sign! Jazzica thought, struggling to retain her normally superior awareness. *It is the emblem of the crucifixation of Jesus H. Christ, Patronizing Saint of the Christian Dior Church.* She gasped. *Has a Self-Manipulator of Religions been here on Arruckus?*

121

"Now," Spilgard said, "touch your nose, woman."

The vast gathering of Freedmenmen held its breath as a single breathholder. Instinct failed to warn Jazzica of the trickiness of the thing; she swiftly brought her hands toward her face, and with a slashing, highly-honed movement put a finger from either hand in her mouth, and eye.

Spilgard turned to face the congregation.

"She is potchkied," he intoned. "It is done."

And the Freedmenmen abruptly cheered in a lusty, ringing voice, raising their arms and leaping about throughout the cavern. Jazzica looked at Spilgard, saw a trace of relief on his face.

"Come with me, girl," said a rough, scratching voice. "We have much to discuss."

Jazzica looked up, and saw the Revved-Up Mother Caramello motioning her to a pair of seats in the rear of the ledge. Between them, on a small table, was a pitcher and two mugs. She nodded and joined the old woman at the table.

"Sit," said the Revved-Up Mother. "And pay attention—"

Jazzica listened as the old woman went on at length about what it meant to be the holy woman of these fierce and disciplined people. As she listened, she drank. And as she drank, a profound change overtook her.

Her head seemed to swim. Her body felt loose, supple. Her timesense slowed, until each moment seemed to pass at a leisurely pace.

She felt marvelous.

Everything's great, she thought. *Yeah.*

122

The Revved-Up Mother Caramello was saying, "—anything that comes into your head, honey. And don't worry—they'll believe it. They want to believe it. It offers them comfort. And don't worry, pretty soon you'll believe it, too. And you'll look up and say, 'I must be going crazy, 'cause I actually believe this stuff I'm saying to them.' And that's when you'll know you're a real Revved-Up Mother."

"Right," Jazzica said, suffused with goodwill toward this old woman. "Absolutely. Right."

"'Course, me," the woman sighed. "—I been hittin' the beer. Oh yeah. Comes with the job, Jazz. The beer, yeah. You'll see. You'll see."

"Oh, I know," Jazzica said, not knowing what she meant but, under the influence of the beer, inexplicably overcome by a poignant sympathy for the woman. "I know."

"You know," the woman said with a lightly mocking tone. "Three mugs and you know. Well, you'll know one day. I'm just glad you got here. I'm old, honey. I'm about ready to go. And there wasn't anybody in the hootch to take my place. If I'd've had a daughter, it would've been her. But it was just boys." She poured a mugful, and with a sudden forceful breath blew off its roiling white head. Jazzica stared, amazed. "You got any kids?" the Revved-Up Mother asked, then gulped a mouthful, swallowed. "Besides the Messiah, I mean?"

"Well," Jazzica allowed herself to allow herself to say. "As a matter of fact, I'm pregnant—"

The woman's face went white. "What? Now?"

Jazzica nodded, giggled, hiccupped lightly.

123

But the Revved-Up Mother Caramello looked grim. She suddenly snatched Jazzica's mug off the table from and dashed the beer from it onto the ground. "You should've told us!" she said sternly. "You can't go 'round quaffing brew with a bun in the oven!" She shook her head. "Well, it's done, anyway. All we can do's hope for the best."

Jazzica looked away, distraught. *What've I done?* she thought.

Then she became aware of a barely-perceptible sensation of otherness, seeming to radiate from within her yet seeking contact with her brew-heightened consciousness.

My daughter! she thought suddenly. *The child within me is a girl!*

Yet how could she know such a thing?

Somehow the knowledge manifested itself in the mind of her brain, the datum exposing its meaning to her suds-brimmed awareness out a who-knows-where-it-comes-from nowhere place.

By Wolfgang's puck! she thought. *This beer gives one tremendous mental powers!*

Jazzica tried to focus her awareness on the presence within, to narrowcast comfort and apology to it. *I'm sorry, my poor unformed daughter,* she thought. *I imbibed a consciousness-altering agent and exposed your fragile prenatal awareness to its mood-modifying effects.*

And from that indistinct point somewhere within, Jazzica thought she sensed a tiny response of love-comfort, and a thought-impression of: *I forgive you.*

But I have placed you at risk, she thought, *and*

124

subjected you to possible intrauterine psychic trauma and physiological aberration.

No problem, came the reply-within. *Absolutely. No problem. More beer.*

From the main floor of the cavern, Pall saw his mother and the Revved-Up Mother Caramello come to the edge of the ledge and look out over the massed tribe. Spilgard joined them, held up his hands.

"Let Jazzica of the Weirdness pronounce the blessing," he said, and gestured to Jazzica.

She stepped forward as the crowd was hush.

"Let the tribe bend elbow," she said. "Let there be commencement of the rolling of the good times."

Pall heard a voice at his side say, "Your mother is the new Revved-Up Mother, Assol."

He whirled, saw Loni standing there, her elfin mouth and generous face the same mouth and face she had had previously.

"Yes," he said.

My mother plays a dangerous game, as usual, he thought in his own private code, which he used for thinking things to himself. *She had better not "blow" this for us, or we are doomed!*

Then he was surprised to find Loni clutching him by the arm and dragging him forward to where the brewmasters were pouring and distributing the beer.

"Come, Assol," she said. "Time it is for cold frosties."

They reached the mug-wumps and brewmasters, were each given a full mug.

"Steak for dinner sometime soon," Loni said, handing him a full mug and clicking the rim of hers against

125

it. She drank deep, gasped, and smacked her lips. "Ah. Primo brewski."

Pall hesitated, then drank.

Once again the chill tang of the liquid assailed him, and the lightheadedness he had experienced during his first taste of the beer returned. He was aware of much commotion around him, and realized that the entire tribe was drinking.

"C'mon, Assol, let's play," Loni urged, tugging at his arm.

She dragged Pall through clusters of drinking, roistering Freedmenmen. Many waved at him as they passed, holding up a raised fist and crying, "Mauve'Bib! All right!" or "Laserium al-Dilah'! Yeah!"

All offered Pall a mugful of beer.

I have never this much drunk this much before, he thought as he elbowbent his fifth mug. *What'll it . . . do? To . . . um . . . me?*

They left the cavern and moved through a series of passages until they came to a private chamber. Loni led Pall in, let fall the beercloth curtain that was the room's only seal. The din and heat of the massed tribe were a distant thing.

Loni sat on the edge of a beermattress and looked at Pall. "The tribe believes you to be the Laserium al-Dilah'," she said. "Is it so?"

Now is the first test, Pall thought. "I am something more, Loni," he said. "I am . . . the Kumkwat Haagendasz."

She smiled, as though to a crazy person, murmured, "That's nice . . ."

126

"You don't believe me?"

"I do!" she protested. "It's just . . . I know not what such a thing is." She shrugged apologetic. "But I am sure it is a holy thing, Assol. Else why would you be it? You are ours. The legend is fulfilled, more or less."

Pall sensed a nexus-node at that event-juncture. A series of possible futures presented itself, and he had to choose. Some entailed a careful marshalling of his unique Boni Maroni culinary abilities. Others required the use of sheerest fraud.

Yet all had a thing in common—they meant ascension to power among the Freedmenmen, and contained within their dynamic the possibility of shutting his mother up and showing her he could make it on his own.

Oh, he knew her plan: he was to recruit the Freedmenmen tribes in the service of House Agamemnides, then overthrow House Hardchargin and get back in business.

But what then? A life of fear of conquest by the next Great Big House capable of allying with the Emperor and his Hardehaurhar?

Pall shook his head.

No, he thought. *Businesses come and go, and their emergences and dwindlings're as the waxing and waning of the moons. Religions stay around forever, tax-exempted to boot. What could be better than an organization where the consumer blames himself for product failure?*

Pall then revelated that, merely by proclaiming himself a thing—Mahdl-T, Laserium al-Dilah', Kumkwat Haagendasz, King of the Potato People—he would in

127

fact become it. The desire of the Freedmenmen for a savior was such that, by now, it would be difficult for him to prove that he was not the one they sought. He was the right man-child at the right place-location at the right time-moment—to become, for these people, their Messiah.

Who in his right mind-brain could then be content with the family business?

Yet there must be the having of a gimmick, he thought. *A thing to mark my coming, and the emergence of my Freedmenmen from obscurity into power. A dessert—for it must be that, given the severe restrictions of Arruckus's resources—to top all desserts.*

And the answer came to him in a single word.

Liqueur.

Beer liqueur! he thought. *Great Maida's Heater! It's a natural!*

"You're so quiet, Assol," Loni said. "Why?"

He smiled. "Liqueur," he said. "Made from beer. With all this sugar around here? It cannot miss."

"When you talk like that, Assol, I grow frightened," she said.

Perfect, he thought. *As though it were a sacramental thing—beer liqueur, the dessert of desserts, made only on Arruckus. As used by the Freedmenmen in their savage-but-beautiful rituals, and so forth and on-so.*

Needs a naming, though . . .

"Loni," Pall said gently. "What would you name a liqueur made from beer?"

"A . . . liqueur?" she asked. "A cordial thing?"

"Yes."

128

And the girl-child paused a moment in thought-trance, then said, "Benedictdoon?"

Pall sighed. "No, my sugar baby."

"Assol, what is this you speak of? Liqueur—from the brew of Schmai-gunug?"

And he began to tell her of his concept-plan: that one day Arruckus, the dessert planet, would be transformed. There would be liqueur, and profits, and from these, there would be arable soil for the cultivation of produce. There would be pastureland and forageturf for the raising of livestock.

There would, in a word, be entrees.

"And you will lead us to that time, Assol?" she asked softly.

"Oh, yes," Pall said. "Oh, yes."

book three

THE PROFIT

"You feel you know me—my methods, my techniques, my proclivities. Yet I tell you that you know nothing. I am the ultimate mystery, the supreme never-can-be-known. You say to me, 'Mauve'Bib, here is a garlic press.' Yet I tell you that I am He Who Lives By The Knife And The Fist. I place the flat blade of my knife on the unpeeled clove. Down upon it I smash my fist. The garlic is crushed; its skin flakes off.

"Now go away, I'm in a bad mood."

—from "Reply to the Boni Maroni Council on Herbs and Spices," as reprinted in "The Portable Mauve'Bib," edited by the Princess Serutan

"A - h - h - h - h - h - h - h - h - h - h - h - h - h - h - h - h - h - h - h - h - h - h - h - h - h - h - h - h - h - h - h, my dear nephew," the Baron Vladimir Hardchargin sighed. "Do come in."

Filp-Rotha, shanana-Baron of House Hardchargin and Vice-President, General Manager, and Supreme Maitre d' of the Shadvlad Rendezvous, showed only the slightest hesitation before entering the day chamber of his uncle. *He's exercised over something, the pig,* thought the young man. *Else why summon me here?*

"You think I am exercised about something, Filp," the Baron said. "Else why would I, the Baron Vladimir Hardchargin, summon you all the way here, to the planet Getty Premium, home world of I, your uncle, the Baron Vladimir Hardchargin, who, in fact, is me?"

"Yes, Uncle."

The Baron was seated on an electrolux recliner, his massive flabby bulk overlapping its confines. He wore an ostentatious robe of rare smoked sable, inset with szelma diamonds and trimmed with precious holi-

133

mack'rl sapphires. To the side, looking on impassively, sat the Mantan, Peter De Vries.

"Tell me, Filp," the Baron drawled. "How long have you been in charge of the Shadvlad Rendezvous—the planet formerly known as Arruckus, or Doon, the Dessert Planet?"

"Ever since the ousting of Lotto and the completion of Jonzun Fillup's design scheme, Uncle," Filp-Rotha said warily. "Two years."

"Whose scheme?"

The youth said testily, "Pardon me—the scheme you collaborated on with Jonzun Fillup."

With sudden sharpness the Baron snapped, "The scheme I *gave* Jonzun Fillup. His contribution was minor. Minor!"

"Yes, sir."

"Two years." The Baron pursed his spittle-gleaming flubby-tubby lips and touched his fingertips together. *Can it truly be that long?* he thought. *Ah-h-h, but time flies when you're ruthlessly wielding subtle treachery in quest of ultimate power.*

With sudden ferocity, he lashed out, "And why, in those two years, have you been unable to suppress the Freedmenmen scum and bring under control the pretzels?"

"But they are under control, Uncle," the young man protested. "The number of pretzels at large shrinks daily. And business is good. I'm booked with conventions through next summer."

The Baron outwardly frowned but smiled inwardly at himself, saying nothing outwardly out loud but thinking

134

silently to himself: *Excellent. He identifies himself with the lounge. This suits my fell scheme utterly.*

"Business is adequate," the Baron said. "And adequate is not good." He shook his head. "Do not insult my intelligence, Filp. Surely you know I have my own sources of information."

Spies! thought Filp-Rotha, mentally leaping up and down in a rage. *Spies within spies within spies! And those spies, spying on other spies within spies! Very well. I must be subtle in my own treachery, lest mine own devious art in mine own face up-blow.*

"Ye-e-e-e-s, of cour-r-r-s-e," he breathed.

"You think I send against you spies," the Baron said with a little smile. "But of a certainty, I spies against you send. And what do my spies tell me? That the Freedmenmen presently run about the planet virtually unchecked. It's not bad enough that they interdict our supplies of beer and make it difficult—and expensive— for us to keep the bars supplied. No, now they have begun to siphon off our dessert trade with renegade pastry wagons of their own!"

Filp-Rotha tried to swallow in a dry throat. "There has been some illegal smuggling of pastry, Uncle," he said. "But—"

"Some! I'm told you can be trampled to death in the rush of our patrons whenever their little doughnut carts come by!"

"But—"

"Silence!" The Baron suddenly sat back and collected himself. In a voice of utter calm (and *that* coursed fear through his nephew more than his outbursts of rage) he said, "Surely I need not remind you how undesirable such an arrangement is. When patrons rush pell-mell for Freedmenmen desserts, they leave the lounges. They stop drinking. They abandon the pretzels we have taken such pains to supply them with. They render our own pastry chefs redundant. We lose customers. We lose reputation. We lose money!"

The fat man sat back and adjusted the folds of his robe in irritation. Filp-Rotha looked at De Vries, but got only a slightly raised eyebrow in reply.

He can't speak to me that way, the youth thought. *I'm all he's got. Who'll he get to replace me? The schnauzer?*

"You think I am wrong to speak to you thus," the Baron said. "But consider, my headstrong nephew: we are not in this alone. Our partner is for the time content to remain silent. He shall prove a most implacable opponent should his patience wear thin." The Baron threw a sideways glance at the youth. "His patience, that is, with you, dear boy."

Filp-Rotha's face flickered an iota of disquiet. "You would never abandon me to the Emperor!" he hissed.

"Would I not?" quoth the Baron. "We are in the restaurant business! The most cutthroat industry in the known universe! The stakes are too high for appeals to petty familial loyalty, Filp." Abruptly his manner changed, growing relentful, soothing, and giving-the-other-guy-a-break. "Now, tell me about the Freedmenmen."

"They have a new religious leader," Filp-Rotha said. "They call him Mauve'Bib. It means, 'One who wears a purple napkin.' "

"Well, find him. Remove him from his position of power. Offer him a job opening for Sammy."

"He cannot be found, Uncle." *You fool*, thought the youth. *You think that the ultimate coin for commerce in loyalty. Not everyone desires to open for Sammy, Uncle—how little you understand human nature.*

"Then perhaps our partner can be of some help," the Baron mused. "No doubt a few squadrons of his Hardehaurhar should be able to root out and dispose of this Freedmenmen problem. Now, as to the pretzels—"

"Our progress in capturing them is hampered by the Freedmenmen," Filp-Rotha said. "Many of my hunters return from the wilds intoxicated. There are rumors—"

The Baron sat forward suddenly, alert. "Yes? Go on."

"Er . . . nothing, Uncle." *Damn my impulsiveness!* Filp-Rotha thought.

"Continue, nephew. There are rumors . . ."

The young man hesitated, said, "Some of those who return from hunting the pretzels speak of an . . . experiment . . . being conducted by the Freedmenmen out in the wilds."

The Baron's eyes narrowed in the fat pockets of their sockets. "What sort of experiment?"

"They are apparently trying to produce . . . a liqueur. Distilled from beer."

The Baron's eyes abruptly ceased their glitter. He stared *at* his nephew and spoke *to* him. "Can they?" he husked.

"We don't know," the young man said. "It's possible."

The Baron sat back. *Think on it!* he thought on it. *Beer-quintessence! What a prize! Isn't the known universe filled with all manner of insipid cordials and liqueurs, of everything from honeydew melon to yogurt? Yet is there not none of beer? What genius thought of this? I have sore underestimated these Freedmenmen . . .*

"This wants subtlety, Filp," the Baron said. "We must move against the Freedmenmen enough to shut down their dessert operations, yet permit them sufficient leeway to continue the experiments with the liqueur. Once they have perfected it, we shall move in and take it."

Ah-h-h, Filp-Rotha thought. *He*—

"You think ah-h-h," the Baron drawled. "Be not so quick to think ah-h-h-h, to congratulate yourself, nephew. The capture of the pretzels is still your responsibility. I shall be keeping close scrutiny on your success. After all . . ." The Baron permitted himself to twinkle his eye wryly. "I myself have a responsibility—to report to my partner, His Sublime Impressiveness, the Emperor Shaddap IV. He must be updated continuous in re the competence of our manager on Arruckus."

Very well, silently thought Filp-Rotha to himself. *Threaten me with the Emperor. I'll play the dutiful maitre d' for now. But some day . . . some day . . .*

"You are thinking some day, some day," the Baron said coolly. "I suggest you think instead on a new name we might give the beer liqueur. Tell me, Filp—and you, too, Peter—what think you on Brewhaha? Too Irish?"

What else can one say about the Universe, except that it's the greatest?

—from "Mauve'Bib's Thousand-and-One Sure-Fire Banquet Jokes," edited by the Princess Serutan

Pall-Mauve'Bib knew he had drunk a large quantity of the beer the night before. But the edges of that mental datum feathered off into thinnings of indistinction in the deeptrained fuzzbundle of his mind. There was only the clear memory of Spilgard, Shashlikh, Rathham, and a few other tribal chiefs sitting around Council table, drinking. That, and something about a belching contest.

Volume, duration, and "creativity" had been tested. And even as he had made the chamber resound with stentorian detonations of beersound, Pall could feel the stern gaze of the Freedmenmen upon him.

It was a contest he had had to win.

And, marshalling his superior abilities, focussing his hyperawareness on the immediate necessity-choice-tactic to belch with ultimate loudness, he had succeeded.

They respect me now, he thought, sitting up in bed, temples pounding with hangover headthrob. *Or have I dreamed all this?*

He swung out of the bed, feet hitting the cold rock-candy floor. Pain winced through his stomach muscles—a somatic remnant of another event in realtime, dense with meaning, and evoking the sharp mental image of himself that just-completed night prior.

He'd risen with contained desperation, yet quietly, that he might leave undisturbed the asleep Loni at his side. Now, in present morning-time, he thought back to that previous hour, saw himself tiptoeing in delicate balletings to the ablution chamber. There, amid the stark hush of the hootch slumbering its deepest pre-dawn rest, instinct warned Pall to give his *self* over to the tides churning powerful within himself that demanded self-cleansing. This he did, and heaved his beerguts.

There had been much of this of late—hours spent far out on in unto the night, festive in imbibement and bon-hommie-filled with raucous merry hoo-hah. Hootch-leaders had come from erg and eek, from dork and freen, from every point of the Great Blab.

Yet there was a deeper motive behind these gatherings than mere pleasure.

He had spoken of it to his mother the day before.

He had visited her in her chambers, once those of the Revved-Up Mother Caramello, their walls covered with beercloth hangings of patterns depicting myths and legends out of the Freedmenmen's rich cultural history, folklore, and anthropology.

"You drink too much with the help," Jazzica'd chid, making of her voice a nagging thing.

"It's necessary, Mother," he'd said.

"But . . . why?" she'd objected. "They already accept your leadership. Make yourself too familiar with them, and you run the risk of devaluing the coin of your authority."

"We speak of a mere few beers with the guys, Mother."

"No few beers're mere, no group of subordinates guys," she'd warned. "It's no way to run a business."

His eyes, their original brown now utterly hid by the beer-imbued red-on-red, 'd burned bright into hers. "I am not running a business," he'd whispered. "I am doing something larger."

She'd blanched deathly white at a sudden comprehension of the import of his speaking. "Pall!"

"You see now, Mother?" he'd hissed. "I must complete my task. Am I the Mahdl-T? I am. Am I the Laserium al-Dilah'? I am. Am I the Messiah . . . ?"

Then she'd stood and pointed at him a finger dramatic. "You—"

"—play a dangerous game? Perhaps." He'd turned on his beerheel and stopped at the doorway. Whirling to face her, he'd said, "It's a game I'll win. I have no desire to go through life a loser."

"You speak coldly harsh."

"Thus you yourself taught me."

"And what of the teachings of your father?" she'd challenged. "Did he instruct you to sabotage the raw materials of your competitors?"

Pall shot her a glancing look. She referred, he knew, to a practice he had authorized some months before: sending squads of Freedmenmen brewworkers out to the pre-beer pools, and diluting the beer with water. Pastry commandoes and doughnutmen reported from the cities widespread dissatisfaction with the diluted brew. Even the Schlepping Guild, normally secretive, had begun to voice complaint . . .

"My father is machoola," he said. "Thus're the ways of business unpredictable and rife with the deadliest

141

peril. I choose a way more ambitious. It'll assure security both financial and social when I'm through.''

She'd protested the more, voicing a woman's fears of the danger he'd court by setting himself up as the sole and divine leader of this fierce and wild people. But he'd silenced her with a belch, said, "My generation is more practical than yours. We want it all: money, power, career, family, and membership in certain exclusive health clubs.''

Now Pall dressed, hearing Loni stir, and thought: *I have drunken of the beer. The eye of the Egad is upon me. I am expert in the ways of burpnoise and gutspuke. I am Freedmenmen in all ways save one.*

He put on his sweatsuit and went out into the hootch. As always, a small band of men silently joined him, hovering close to his every move. These were the Feydeaukin, the so-called Farcees, humor-commandoes whose sacred and sworn duty it was to protect the person of Mauve'Bib, or die laughing.

"Good morning, Assol.''

It was Spilgard, leaning against the doorway of his chamber, his form girt in his nightrobe of beer-terrycloth.

The nabe looked sickly wan, said: "My head is hung over as the moons above the sugars.'' It was ritual Freedmenmen greeting following a sudsfest, a night of drinking. "Were I to drop dead this moment, it were a blessing of Schmai-gunug.''

Pall replied ritualistically, "Let Spilgard take aspirin.''

"I took.''

142

"Let him gulp fizzpowder of bromo."

"I gulped."

"Let him drink coffee."

"I drank."

"Then, Spilgard," Pall said, completing the ritual, "have a beer."

"Good idea."

The nabe disappeared into his chamber, returned a moment later with a full mug. He bent elbow and quaffed, smacked his lips, said, "Forgive me, Mauve'Bib, but there is talk among the people. It is of your sister."

Pall nodded. He knew the girl-child was a source of unease among the men-adults and women-grownups of the hootch. "What say the people about my sister, Nailya?" he asked.

"Many call her Nailya-the-Totally-Weird, Mauve' Bib," the nabe confessed. "And, truth, she gives even me the beercreeps. Her manner is not that of ordinary children."

"She is quiet," Pall said guardedly-yet-agreeingly. "What in that should fearful Spilgard?"

"She speaks a language no man has ever heard," Spilgard said. "'Melt 2 Tbls. butter, cook ½ c. chopped onion till soft.' What inhuman tongue be this, Mauve'Bib?"

Pall held up his hand to assuage the nabe's disquiet. *I have expected this difficulty,* he thought. *And now it is here. How can I explain to this proud, unsophisticated man that my sister, because my mother drank beer and ate cocktail mix while her daughter was still in-womb,*

143

was born in full conscious possession of all the recipes of
her female ancestors over hundreds of generations? It's
an unusual thing.

"It is mere child-babble," Pall said. "Let us not continue to waste time on it. Come, I have need of your wisdom and strength for a more important task."

The nabe looked suddenly sober, and with a subtle trace of foreboding asked, "You are ready for the test?"

"I am ready."

The Freedmenmen chief nodded with abrupt decisiveness, drank the last of the beer, slammed his mug down on a nearby table. "Hal printz! At last! Let us summon the others."

And Spilgard led the way through the hootch, collecting a band of senior warriors and council members to witness the test of this day, when Pall-Mauve'Bib would ride the pretzel, and become full-Freedmenmen entire, already.

He had mounted with others on raids, riding salt boulder on pretzelback after men experienced in sugarriding had summoned the Brewer and brought it under control. But he knew that in Freedmenmen tradition a boy became a man only after riding Schmaigunug solo. This was a rite of passage he himself must make. Else all his life, he'd be prey to a devastating question he'd be unable to answer—If you're the Messiah, how come you can't ride a pretzel?

Such an omission on my resume could hold the deadliest peril for the game-plan, Pall thought.

They gathered in an area of raw sugar several

kilometers from the hootch. Pall noticed that the men kept their distance from him, glance-shooting him with watchful looks.

Spilgard stepped forward, his face a mask of ritual solemnity. "Curse our enemies from now till the Twelfth of Never," he said. "They denied us the Hajj-Pajj."

Pall replied as he had been instructed. "Come," he said. "Let us punch them in their nose."

"I, Spilgard, am Nabe," Spilgard continued. "I would greatly love to punch them in their nose. But I am so damn busy, I can't get away from the office."

"I will go," Pall replied. "No, don't get up, Spilgard the Nabe. I will go."

"Are you sure."

"Yes, I am sure."

"I can get to it tomorrow," Spilgard intoned.

"No, no, no problem," Pall said.

"Then, Assol, who is Pall-Mauve'Bib, thanks."

"You're welcome."

The first ritual exchange was done. Now another Freedmenman stepped forward, said to Pall, "They live far from hootch. How will you get to them, Assol?"

Pall announced to the troop, "I will summon a Brewer. I will ride the wild pretzel."

The ceremonial exchange had ended. Spilgard looked into Pall's eyes and said, in the deeper-warmer-nicer tones of friendship, "Ride the bastard, Assol."

Shashlikh approached him with two long beermetal devices, asked, "One lumper or two?"

They'll take it as cowardice if I choose one, Pall

145

thought. *Yet two could precipitate accusations of big shot.*

"Two," Pall said.

Approval mumured among the men. Shashlikh handed him both of the rodlike devices, as the Freedmenmen flurried in anticipation.

Here goes no thing, Pall thought.

He strode out onto the copper-streaked flat of white/brown sugar melange. Finding a suitable spot of open ground, he drove the stake of the first lumper into the topsugars, anchoring it firmly. A spring-wound packer, when released, would compress scoops of sugar into small cubes. The resulting noise and disturbance would transmit swiftly through the ground, serving as an irritant to any large pretzels in the area and luring them to investigate. The sugar cubes would be collected afterwards by the children, for use in beercoffee and beertea and other beerbeverages.

He released the packer.

"Lump! . . . lump! . . . lump!"

He paced off a few steps and drove the other lumper into the ground, released its packer after a moment's hesitationing.

"Lump! . . . lump! . . . lump! . . ."

"Lump! . . . lump! . . . lump! . . ."

Pall looked around, and noted that the others seemed to have vanished. As always he marvelled at the uncanny ability of Freedmenmen to live within these sugars, making of themselves a hidden, indistinguishable thing in the natural surround. Spilgard, Shashlikh, and the rest had virtually disappeared, scattered across the landscape, somehow managing to blend their brightly-hued sweatsuits with the brown-and-white streaked sugarplain.

Then Pall second-glanced, and his hyper-trained superduper awareness detected a dot-flurrying in the distance. It was Spilgard and the other men, running like hell for the hootch, tiny specks against the unforgiving if sweet terrain.

And the lesson of Spilgard came back to Pall.

"Do not plant your lumpers too close together," the nabe'd said. "They create a mutual seismic reinforcement, increasing the amplitude of the signal. The Brewer they'll summon'll be too large for mounting."

That is why they have run, he thought. *But it is too late now.*

And Pall waited, his Boni Maroni–trained awareness focussed with razorlike precision on the fact that he had messed up.

Politics is a subtle thing—this all men know. Yet there is a subtler thing than even that: thumb-wrestling. Inherent in its practice are subtleties within subtleties within subtleties. From this we may learn much of the ultimate essence that pervades widespread ubiquitous all over the place.

—from "'Aroogah! Aroogah!': Arruckus Arising," by the Princess Serutan

The Baron Vladimir Hardchargin adjusted his la-zer-boy recliner beams and signalled for food. Only when it had been brought—dakota figs from North Kadota, heavy dates with a hot chick—did he turn to the Mantan, Peter De Vries.

"You think I was too harsh with Filp-Rotha, Peter," the Baron said.

The Mantan shrugged casual. "Not really."

"No, no, do not try to dissemble me," the Baron insisted. "You think me too dictatorial. But what you do not know, and what my nephew does not know, is that my relationship with my dear silent partner is not all it should be."

"Indeed?" De Vries said. "I thought the Emperor was satisfied with the success of the Shadvlad."

"Satisfied is not the word," the Baron chortled, his chubby wattles quivering gelatinous. "He is amazed. The place is doing good business. We're in all the magnetazines. Did you see the spread in *Cosmospolitan*? They loved my design for the central banquette."

Jonzun Fillup's design, you mean, thought De Vries. "Oh?" he said. "Then why is Shaddap displeased?"

"Peter, Peter, you assume discord results from failure, when in fact it more often arises from success," the Baron murmured. "Our Emperor, Shaddap IV, has grown ambitious. He now wants total control of the Shadvlad Rendezvous. He has let it be known he suspects me of plotting against him, as part of a plan he ascribes to me to expand the business."

"What . . . plan?"

The Baron tittered. "He believes I intend to franchise the formula all over the universe, and standardize the creation of ten thousand Shadvlads from Bela

148

Tegeuse 3 to Aldebaran. And, do you know, Peter . . ." The Baron paused, flicked his thinning-to-the - point - of - almost - not - really - being - there - at - all eyebrows, whispered, "He is correct!"

"You'd dare?" De Vries said, shocked. "You'd actually try to muscle out the Emperor?"

"He's doubtless planning a similar fate for me!" the fat man snapped. "This is business, Peter—a marriage of convenience. And marriages of convenience can be annulled, should either party cast a longing eye toward the mistress of the partner's secret dreams of affection when . . . anyway, you know what I mean."

De Vries thought a moment, said, "How can you accomplish it? Shaddap is powerful—I refer, not only to his Hardehaurhar, but to his lawyers. After all, he keeps on retainer the law planet of Cravitz Swine."

"NOAMCHOMSKI will support me in a showdown with Shaddap," the Baron stated. "The Great Big Houses fear his power. And I have a secret weapon."

"Money?"

The Baron smirked-chuckled-snorted, sighed, belched, sneezed, twitched, scratched, said, "Pah, money! What I have is more valuable than money. With it I may purchase certain services money cannot."

De Vries's eyes widened as he grasped the man's gist. "You mean—!"

"Precisely." The Baron smiled. "Beer."

The Mantan frowned. Here was intrigue for a thousand Byzantinings! "But how—"

"Think, Peter!" the Baron squealed. "The Schlepping Guild! They live for beer. They will not work without it. Have you ever spoken to a Guild spaceman? Rude, crude, barely domesticated thugs, yes. But: diehard individualists. I have seen them in the bar after a long haul. They would kill a man for a beer. Who controls the brew can call the tune to which the Guild will dance. And who controls the Guild may dictate terms to the Emperor. Whence commerce without transport? Whither NOAMCHOMSKI—Neutralis Organizational Abba Mercantile Condominium Havatampa Orthonovum Minnehaha Shostakovitch Kategorical Imperative—without the Guild's 'Ighliners? Be certain, Peter: beer is power."

"But—" Comprehension dawned in the face of De Vries. "Clever, my Lord Baron," he said. "Yet there remains the problem of the Freedmenmen."

"Precisely," the Baron spat. "That is why it is essential Filp-Rotha see to that nuisance immediately. They must be wiped out—but only after we obtain the recipe for their beer liqueur. Who in the universe could stand against me, were I in possession of that magic fluid?"

"What if your nephew cannot root them out? Arruckus is large, and the expense of mounting a full-scale campaign would be enormous. Not to mention the difficulty of keeping it a secret from the Emperor."

"I have a better idea," the Baron smiled. "Let Filp wreak havoc there for a period. Then I shall move in, curb his cruelty, and propose to their Mauve'Bib the one thing he will find irresistible."

"An alliance?"

"Fa-a-a! Alliance!" the Baron roared with audible

150

contempt. "No, no, this Mauve'Bib is a zealot. He wants no alliance. He wants confrontation. And confrontation he shall have. I intend to challenge him."

De Vries paled, gasped, "You cannot mean bake-off!" He stammered for comprehension. "But . . . why should he agree?"

"He will think it a way to defeat and embarrass me," the Baron said. "The very invitation will flatter the fool."

"But if he wins?" the Mantan posed. "One hears intelligence reports from Doon that the Freedmenmen are expert pastry cooks. After all, living on the sugars—"

"But, my dear Peter, he *will* win."

De Vries stared as the import of the Baron's words impacted his mind. "By Wolfgang's puck!"

"You begin to grasp the scheme, I see," the Baron chortled. "This Freedmenmen messiah will compete against our chefs, all of whom will have been sub-hypnotically prepared to bungle. He will defeat us. We will cry foul, and produce witnesses who will swear that Mauve'Bib is in league with the Emperor. We will seize him and exterminate his Freedmenmen. Shaddap, meanwhile, will protest, backed by his Hardehaurhar. The Boni Maroni will align themselves with the Imperium. We shall appeal to the Great Big Houses, file a grievance with NOAMCHOMSKI, and claim the Emperor is seeking to oust me. That will be our pretext; House Pancakes and House Dressing will rally to my side, depose Shaddap, and institute a tripartite alliance of power. NOAMCHOMSKI will object, the Guild will call foul, the Boni Maroni will cry wolf, and the Great Big Houses will holler—"

"Uncle."

The Baron whirled. Filp-Rotha stood in the doorway, carefully concealing a look of unconcealed contempt.

"Ah, Filp," the Baron rumbled. "You are ready to depart for Arruckus. Splendid. You'll remember our little chat today, I trust?"

"Certainly, Uncle."

You loathsome pig.

"Good, Filp. See to that Freedmenmen problem for me, won't you?"

"Of course."

Filp-Rotha bowed cursorily and strode from the *hall. I shall indeed,* he thought. *Nothing would give me more pleasure than to persecute and decimate a nomadic society of tribal enclaves loosely bound in a planetary confederation by culture, law, and tradition.*

Nothing, that is, except one thing.

The youth smiled treacherous to himself.

To see my face on every bottle, can, and six-pack of beer in the universe!

There should be a word-tension for "fated," conveying a meaning opposite from a thing destined to be. There should also be a garnish-tension for "parsley," denoting the opposite of the leafy herb. Oh, we speak in daily discourse of "anti-parsley," but that is another thing entire. What the word for a thing is can consequent much.

—from "Mauve'Bib Has Ideas and Speaks Them,"
edited by the Princess Serutan

Jazzica noted her own thoughts in her own mind all by herself. *Today Pall rides the wild pretzel. What'll ensue from this?*

And an answer came to her unbidden, a bird of ideation flown right into the middle of her head out of that mental nowhere-which-is-somewhere from which concepts originate in cooperation with the human brain: *He' will use such skill for staging raids on Hardchargin pretzel patrols, likely. That, or neglect duty, and indulge with other teen-men of the hootch in the bombing around.*

The notions were sobering. Either scenario would expose her son to the deadliest peril.

She permitted herself a small sigh. Such preoccupations had no place in the mind of a Revved-Up Mother. There was much work to be done—classes to be taught, dishes to be developed. The dessert raids on the Shadvlad had brought great success, but Filp-Rotha had doubled his corps of bouncers and given them carte blanche in the use of force. Just yesterday had come an incident of violence. Three salesmen, Yadda, D'Dadda, and Sh'boom, had been severely shoved while attempting to move a load of caramel-coated nuggets.

We must accelerate our refinement of the liqueur, she thought. *Else Hardchargin chefs might discover it for themselves. Indeed, they may have spies among us already. Even the most loyal may be tempted by the lure of offworld entrees.*

A knock sounded on the wall of the entrance to her sleep-space. It was Harrumf, Pall's half-wife.

Jazzica greeted her in the customary Freedmenmen manner. "Frisco legit b.o. zooms? How does this day find you?"

Harrumf answered with equal formality. "Par epic preems to ho-hum H'wood. This day finds me well." She hesitated, stopped hesitating, said, "Forgive me, Your Revved-Uppedness. But I am troubled, disturbed."

Jazzica's eyes widened in horror-fear. "Pall!" she gasped. "Is he . . . ?"

"Mauve'Bib rides the Brewer today," Harrumf said simply. "He will not fail."

Jazzica examined the woman before her. Harrumf had become her son's responsibility after Pall'd bested Janis and sent him into exile. Yet Jazzica knew that Harrumf didn't share her son's bed.

"What brings you here, Harrumf?" Jazzica asked.

"There is . . . discontent, Your Revved-Uppedness," the woman said. "Many of the young men are restless. They know Mauve'Bib rides Schmaigunug this day. If he succeeds he will be Freedmenmen-entire. The young men want . . ." She trailed off, uncertain of her mandate to complete the gist of her nub.

"Yes, Harrumf," Jazzica prompted. "They want . . . ?"

"They want Mauve'Bib to fire Spilgard," she said with a straining. "They want him to lead all the tribes in razzmatazzia against the hated Hardchargins, in a final apocalyptic cookoff. They say . . ."

"Yes, Harrumf? They . . . say what?"

She took a deep breath, said, "They say that with the liqueur we shall be invincible."

The room fell silent. Out in the hootch Jazzica heard the sugar rasping its noise on the rough floor as these strange people, so different from those she had known as a child, lived.

They are impatient, she thought. *Word of the beer liqueur has ignited them like a faggot. They believe now that we cannot lose. Twenty generations of quality flans and caramels is suddenly no longer enough.*

"I daren't become involved," Jazzica said. "I'm the hootch's Revved-Up Mother. My task's strictly specified—to bring succor to the tribe, to consecrate the necessary rituals, and to think of a name for the liqueur. All else'd be folly—or worse."

"And've you had any luck, Reverend Mother?" Harrumf asked.

"Some luck, but that poor," Jazzica admitted. "Two names've I come up with—Lagerheads and Doonsbeery." Her voice was a disgusted thing. "I deem them unsatisfactory."

"We should let *Him* decide," Harrumf said suddenly.

This disquieted Jazzica. She worried lest the powers ascribed to Pall be inflated beyond reason, making him god-like, like a god. "Would you deny me my right, Harrumf?" she asked.

The woman looked apologetic, said, "Such was not my intention, Your Revved-Uppedness. I only meant—"

They were interrupted by a rustle at the entrance to

155

the room. A small girl-child, having in age two year-times, stood there.

"Nailya," Jazzica said, greeting her daughter. "Have you been behaving yourself?"

The girl stared soberly serious, with solemn green eyes and oval face. She said gravely, "Pre-heat oven to Med. (350°F)."

What've I borne? thought Jazzica.

"Say hello to your mother, Nailya," Harrumf said to the child-girl.

"Add ¼ tsp. basil, ½ tsp. oregano," said Nailya. "Stir."

A sweat-suited man knocked on the doorway, and without waiting for a reply strode into the room. He was powdered and lightly dusted with sugars, his red-on-red eyes fierce in their burning intensity.

"Yes, Shoanuf?" Jazzica asked.

"I return from the sugars, Revved-Up Mother," he replied. "Pall-Mauve'Bib-who-is-Assol has summoned the brewer and makes ready."

Jazzica nodded. *If he succeeds, this day will live forever in legend,* she thought. *If he fails . . .*

She tried to swallow in a dry throat.

—there may be nothing but a few damnable folk songs, of endless repetitive verses, without bridge or chorus.

The thought left her strangely disturbed. "I will be in my chambers," she husked.

Gathering her robes about her, she swept from the room, then swept back in, her deep training revealing, via short-term memory, that she had been in her chambers to begin with.

There can be no religion without hierarchy. Make every man his own priest, and ensues chaos. For then would there be erased the distinction, so crucial to our way of life, between confessing and talking to yourself.

—from "Mauve'Bib's Religious Lectures for Swingin' Lovers," edited by the Princess Serutan

Pall stood tense on the sugars, shading his eyes for first pretzelsight, as the sound of the thing's approach dinned in his ears.

Spilgard's instructions came back to him. "Schmaigunug will come to your lumper after a few minutes. When he approaches you must be as a piece of the landscape. At age twelve, our Freedmenmen boys know how to stand in the relaxed-readiness, moving yet stationary, alertly human yet a natural thing. You, Assol, are older. And you are not Freedmenmen-born. So just hide behind something."

I will hide behind nothing, Pall thought as the lumpers sent their percussive message throughout the eek. *I will stand proud and still, unafraid, like any Fre—*

The pretzel came out of nowhere, the rising tide of sugarswell sweeping before it lifting Pall up off his feet ninety, a hundred meters into the air. He was flung upward amid a storm of sugarcrystals, higher and higher, the tang of beerbreath suffusing throughout, in a hailstorm of rock-candy stones amid deafening pret-

157

zelroar. He fell, hit with a jolt that shuddered his bones.

Atop Schmai-gunug!

He had landed, on his seat, atop a rough translucent-white boulder.

Saltrock! he thought. *The large crystalline deposits of salt that encrust the backs of the mature pretzels. From the size of this rock, I've summoned a very large pretzel indeed.*

He looked around. From his vantaging he estimated he was more than a hundred meters off the ground, moving in a direction away from the hootch. The wind whipped past him as the snack-behemoth drove on in a grinding-gnashing sound of sugarcrunching. Its blunt head was somewhere before and below him, the throbbing stub-tail behind. He had lighted, by luck, upon the crest of the headring of the creature, and was thankful he'd not have to make ringleap frontward, as did many pretzelriders who landed on the tailring.

Then he thought: *Now for the turning.*

From a pocket in his sweatsuit he produced his swysknife, flipped out its largest blade. Working the point under the edge of the saltrock, he pried the boulder up from the shiny brown pretzelskin. Underneath was soft white doughflesh, tender and sensitive.

The pretzel, which had been ploughing through the sugars in quest of the lumpers, reared back with a roar and began to wheel around, more in reflex response than volitional search for the irritant source. When the monster was facing in the direction he wanted, Pall eased the saltrock back into its seat.

The pretzel began to move forward again, in the desired direction.

Pall felt a wild exhilaration seize him. For the first time in his teenaged life, mobility was his. Vast vistas of freedom opened before his mental eye. Times of sport-riding, competitive racing, other cruise-type recreations were with this test-passing accessed to him.

To hell with religion and restaurants! he thought. *Let's ride!*

He set off on a straight line course, out toward the jim-palmeries in the south. The landscape was a subtly-shifting thing: sugar flats merged with cube ranges—blocky, mountainous formations. The air rushed past him in exhilarating windflow.

He had ridden for perhaps a half-hour, giddy with a newfound sense of freedom, when he spied, heading across his path, a dot in the sky.

Orthodontothopter! Pall thought. *Probably smugglers—or Hardchargins!*

As he watched, the 'thopter hovered, landed. Careful to remain concealed by the pretzel, Pall slowed the creature, leaped down onto its central knot as he'd been trained, then jumped off.

As the pretzel charged off back into the wilds, Pall carefully approached the site where the 'thopter had landed, a shallow basin ringed by rock-candy formations. He moved warily, concealing himself behind the translucent crystalline boulders. From the landing site came a sound of activity, and beerslurp.

Smugglers, indeed, Pall thought. He peered over the rocks.

The leader of the band looked up from the hose that snaked from 'thopter tanks into beerpool. "Keep pumping," he told his two men. "We've got company."

He approached the sweatsuit-clad figure that had emerged from the rocks, and feigned sheepishness. "Glad you happened by, friend," he said. "Any idea how to get to 2430 Hole-In-The-Big-Rock Terrace?"

"You've no need to ask fake directions from me, Gurnsey."

The smuggler gaped, started. "Pall?" he gasped. "Is . . . it . . . truly . . . you . . . Pall?"

It happened of its own accord, then, and the two were embracing and blackslapping. Gurnsey pulled back and shook his head.

"They told me you were dead, lad," he said.

"No, Gurnsey," Pall replied. "I'm just in a different field. Religion." And he explained the events of the past two years as his old tutor and friend listened with wonder.

"Today I have rid the pretzel," Pall said. "From this day commences true getting-down-to-business."

"That's fine, lad! Fine!"

"Will you join me, then, Gurnsey?"

The walleyed hunchback looked away. "Well, now, Pallie . . ." he said. "I be a smuggler now. Money's good, and hours're my own."

"But Gurnsey," Pall protested. "You served my father well, and nobly. Now I ask you to serve me thus, too. No man walks who's more loyal than Gurnsey Halvah."

"Loyalty . . . ?" the squat man mused. "It's the real

160

world, Pall. The whole organization's gone. Safire Halfwit's retired, Drunken Omaha's with the Duke God-knows-where . . . it'd not be the same, lad." He slapped Pall on the back. "Nah, you go on with your religion job. It suits you fine. Me, I'll stick to this now. Besides . . ." And here he winked, and chortled, the Gurnsey of old. "It's fun!"

That word, Pall thought, recoiling at the deepest level of his training.

"Very well, Gurnsey," Pall said. "Good luck to you."

"Aye. And to you, lad. Regards to yer Mum."

He waved, and turned away, trotting off to join the other smugglers.

Pall nodded, then set off away from the 'thopter to find a suitable spot for lumperplant. A struggle had begun in his self, a conflict between the lure of the rollicking, carefree life now enjoyed by his old tutor, and the stern demands of his new career.

Fun, Pall thought. *That most dangerous of seductions.*

It was a Path, true enough—a Path toward stagnation and poverty. As by reflex, he tensed to repel the attraction he felt toward it. "Let the inferior of the race prattle about fun," his mother had once told him. "It's the Path of the Loser."

Then, invoking his mother's Boni Maroni discipline, he repeated the Litany Against Fun: *"I must not have fun. Fun is the time-killer. Fun is for children, customers, and the help. I will forget fun. I will take a pass on it. And while it is going, I will turn a blind eye toward it.*

When fun is gone there will be nothing. Only I will remain—I, and my will to win. Damn, I'm good."

Pall felt calmness return, noted with approval his re-heightened awareness of himself and his ambition.

Damn, I'm God, he thought.

He planted the lumper near a patch of bongo wafer, and when a pretzel emerged, mounted it without difficulty. Once more he pried up a saltrock on its back until it began to wheel around. When its head was facing in the direction of Hootch Grabr, Pall replaced the boulder, and the pretzel set off.

A hundred bottles of beer on the wall, a hundred bottles of beer. If one of those bottles should happen to fall, it would shake the very foundations of the Universe.

—from Mauve'Bib's "The Seven Pillows of Wisdom," edited by the Princess Serutan

Pall dismounted the pretzel in full view of the entrance to Hootch Grabr, that Spilgard and the others might see the success of his endeavor. Two children were gamboling in child's play in the shallow basin that served as central entrance/plaza for the hootch. When Pall brought the pretzel to a halt by again lifting the saltrock on its back, the skidding, terror-filled stopping of the creature threw up tidal waves of sugar. One of these engulfed the children, killing them.

I must practice braking, Pall thought.

He was met by the nabe and the council chiefs. Spilgard's red-on-red eyes were admiring and abashed simultaneous.

162

"We fled your badly-placed lumpers, Mauve'Bib," he said. "For that I am ashamed. Yet we did see you ride the brewer, and affirm your passing of the test."

"You did not see me mount?" Pall asked.

"Ah . . . no," Spilgard said.

"Nor did you see me turn the creature, and ride in what direction I willed?"

"Well, we . . . no."

Pall thought: *This is my chance.*

"Then," he said loudly, that the others might hear without effort, "you did not witness my talking with Schmai-gunug?"

Harsh mutterings hissed nearby as the assembled chieftains exchanged excited whispers.

"The legend! He speaks with Schmai-gunug!"

"We did not see this . . . yet it must be so!"

"He is the Messiah!"

Spilgard furrowed his brow, silenced the others with a look, turned back to Pall.

"Mauve'Bib," he said slowly. "We believe you to be the Mahdl-T, the one of Freedmenmen legend whom the Great Prophet Phyllis said would come to drive us to Paradise and back. But the Revved-Up Mother, Jazzica of the Weirdness, tells us that the Great Prophet Phyllis was decanonized, her prophecies discontinued. So be it. We further believe you to be the Laserium al-Dilah', the Bright Light of the Italian Love Song. This we believe even though none of us knows what is your role, or powers, or purpose. So be it. We all believe you to be these things—even Korma believes, and he doesn't believe anything."

163

The nabe looked grave, furrowed his cracked brow in concentration, said, "But did you really talk to Schmai-gunug?"

Pall nodded. "I did."

Spilgard began to tremble. "That I have lived to see this day . . ." he began.

A commotion bustled nearby, and many women arrived. Among these was Jazzica, who forced her way through the crowd to Pall and Spilgard.

"What happens here?" she demanded.

"He is Come, Revved-Up Mother," Spilgard said quietly. "Mauve'Bib this day did ride the pretzel—"

"Excellent," she permitted herself to say, then permitted herself to look at Pall and permitted herself to add, "Congratulations, Pall."

"—and did talk with Schmai-gunug."

A sudden silence fell all over them like a blanket.

"Uh, that's sufficient, Spilgard," Pall interposed with haste. He smiled at his mother, said, "Some of the men are under the impression that—"

"Mauve'Bib did converse this day with Schmai-gunug!" Spilgard cried.

Jazzica looked sharply at Pall. "You spoke with the giant pretzel?"

Pall unflinched in her gaze. "Well . . . yeah . . ."

"And so," she replied in a voice Pall had not heard since he was much younger—anger-mounting, sore exasperated. "I suppose you think that means you're the Messiah?"

Pall looked away, shrugged. "Well . . . right. Yes."

Spilgard turned to the gathering crowd, which by

now numbered in the hundreds, announced, "It is as the prophecy foretold!"

And a great roar of approbation arose from the massed Freedmenmen in Hootch Grabr, and there was joy and celebration. Spilgard held aloft his hands to signal silence.

"Let this day be commemorated for all our history," he declared. "Let there be holiday pan-hootch. Close down beerwork and mugshop. Adjourn schools early and call in the brewworkers. Close down the post office and let there be a white sale in the linen mill. Send word by caltrans to every erg and eek, to the folk of pan and pizza, even to every paine and weber: the Messiah this day has come."

Again the Freedmenmen broke into a mammoth roar, and dispersed throughout the hootch to make ready for the fete. Amid the unbearable frenzy Jazzica turned to Pall.

"By the thousand rooms of Mimi's sheraton!" she swore. "Do you not know that Baron Hardchargin has challenged you to a bakeoff? Is this not the time to marshall these Freedmenmen to regain the business?"

"We shall regain the business, Mother," Pall said. "And oh, so much more. But we shall do it—I shall do it—not as Pall Agamemnides, son of Duke Lotto, but as Pall-Mauve'Bib . . . Messiah!"

She shot a sharp glance at him. "They will expect much from their Messiah."

"I will give them much."

"What can you give them, Pall?"

165

"Power," he said. "Have I not already given them unified leadership? Am I not on the brink of giving them the liqueur? In fact, are you not the One to present me with a name for it, finally?"

Jazzica jerked her head away, abashed. "I have thought on it," she confessed. "Yet nothing grabby did to me come."

His eyes blazed. "Must I do everything around here?" he demanded. "Tell me what you have thus far, Mother."

"Lagerheads," she said softly. "Doonsbeery."

"Fa-a-a-a!"

"Harrumf came up with Grenadoon."

"Ayah! Schmai-gunug could tell me better names than that!"

She looked at him with defiant nostrilflare. "I told you from the beginning this was not my department. Can you do better?"

"Probably."

"Then do so! I must see to your sister."

And Jazzica spun on her beerheel and strode off toward her chambers.

It's a hard thing, this naming of the liqueur, Pall thought. *But vitally necessary. Yet there is a way to send the mind where it may be inspired for the task of the naming.*

Yes, he agreed with himself. *I will eat the cocktail mix and drink the beer. We shall see what names I can come up with. And then we shall be ready to face the Hardchargins, and from them gain vengeance-victory-vanquishment.*

Jazzica sat on a cushion of sugarfilled beerfiber in her alcove, the noise of the celebration a muffled roar without. *Here is irony,* she thought bitterly. *My son is acclaimed hero and savior by an entire people, yet I fret and stew in discontent, fearful of his future and sore cranky over his choice of profession.*

The reason for it, she knew, lay in the Freedmenmen themselves. They were a proud people, with a noble heritage tempered in untold fierce fires of persecution over centuries. Their culture, if narrow, was deep. Theirs was the very embodiment of a life of essentials, all traces of softness, weakness, and frivolity burned long ago to cinder by the harsh necessities of life on Doon. They were resilient, strong, and—within the stern code of survival forced upon them by both man and nature—utterly honorable. Yet, too, they were boring hicks.

Jazzica had grown up on Wallach-Eli, a planet renowned for its sophistication and culture. Her training since early childhood had been in Boni Maroni academies, where exposure to arts liberal had accompanied instruction in cuisine haute.

The result of such an education transcended mere proficiency in the kitchen—Jazzica, like most of her kind, felt herself to be superior to people who knew less than she. It was an assumed thing. Yet it was also a miraculous thing, for, luckily, she felt in no way inferior to people who knew *more* than she.

Now came the prospect, not of regaining the family business and returning to Cowboydan, there to live out her life as the ducal widow with all attendant powers and pleasures, but of remaining here, on Arruckus, Revved-up Mother to a tribe of nomads in sweatsuits.

Pall would cement our tie to these rustics by accepting the religious mantle, she thought. A bitter laugh escaped her. *And I am powerless to stop it. Yet, am I? Yes, I am.* A bitter giggle escaped her and ran after the bitter laugh.

"Excuse me, Revved-Up Mother."

It was Spilgard. He stood at the entrance to her alcove, clad in his in-hootch clothes of loose trousers and slipover shirt of closely-woven beercloth. Jazzica detected about him a feeling-tone of worry.

"What is it, Spilgard?" she queried.

"I seek Mauve'Bib," he replied. "There is word from Arrucksack I would speak into his ear with my mouth. Yet I cannot find him."

"What sort of word comes from the capital?"

"The Baron Hardchargin has arrived," the nabe said. "Yet there is more. Our spies report that the Emperor himself is expected, travelling in retinue with five legions of Hardehaurhar. This'll be no ordinary bakeoff."

"Pall must be told," Jazzica said, gathering her beerrobes about her. "Come, let's look for Loni."

"I have spoke to the girl-child Loni. She knows not where he is."

Jazzica flung him a glance of direst perturbedness, and with a swishing rush of her raiment strode out the doorway. Spilgard followed.

The celebration for the coming of the Messiah had entered its fourth hour, and was dwindling. Hootchwide were Freedmenmen in the drunken state, or asleep, or woozened by the drinking of their brains out on the beer. It took a number of questions and fruitless searches in many chambers and rooms before Jazzica and Spilgard arrived at the Brewer room off the main assembly hall.

Only two westingglobes were alight, throwing stark shadows across the bin in which the cocktail mix was kept, and where the ritual beer pitchers and mugs were carefully stored.

"Why'd Kibbee say Pall'd come here?" Jazzica murmured.

A groan moaned from a nearby source unseen.

Spilgard sprang forward. "Web exex rap FCC!" he oathed. "It is Mauve'Bib!"

Pall was on the floor, behind the cocktail mix bin. With both arms stiff he dragged himself into view.

"Pall!" Jazzica gasped.

"I've done it," Pall said. "I have seen. There is a thing. I have seen a thing . . ."

Spilgard to Jazzica whispered, "He has seen a thing!"

"More!" Pall snapped. Weak with effortfulness, he stood. Half-falling, he leaned against Spilgard for support. "I have done what the Revved-Up Mothers do—eaten of the cocktail mix—"

"Pall!" Jazzica gasped agin.

169

He spun and seized his mother by the shoulders, staring into her eyes with a blazing expression. "I am the Kumkwat Haagendasz, Mother," he said. "And I understand what is happening on Arruckus. The Baron seeks to destroy the pretzels and monopolize the beer. But in so doing he seeks to effect his own doom! The beer is created by the pretzels!"

An abrupt silence exploded with quiet in the chamber.

Spilgard said with uncertain tone, "You did not know this?"

Pall looked at him. "What?"

"All Freedmenmen know of the delicate links of interdependence that unite all life-forms," the nabe said. "Our eight-year-olds are taught such basic ecological principles. Salt makes the brewer die, which creates the nuts, the cocktail mix; the nuts of some of the mix form the nuggets, the young pretzels. Water combines with other nuts of the mix, and with yeast, to form the beer." The gaunt man shrugged. "It wants not an offworld Kumkwat Haagendasz to know this thing."

His self aburn with intensity, Pall stared into the man's eyes. "But tell me, Spilgard," he said. "Do you also know that the brewer nuts, when ground into a paste and mixed with certain oils, yield a delicious, nutritious thing? A thing I call 'peanut butter'? A thing that will assure our triumph in the bakeoff over the Baron and his minions!"

"Pall!" Jazzica continued to gasp. "How do you know this? What do you intend to . . . do?"

170

"I came here some hours ago," he explained. "I wanted to eat the nuts and drink the beer, to see if it would help in devising a name for the liqueur. I drank much beer. And in that state of blotto-awareness I ate many nuts, and it came to me that they could be used and cooked with thus. It just came to me, Mother!" With lowered voice he said, "That is how I know I am the Kumkwat Haagendasz. I am indeed He Whose Fruit-Like Soul Is Tempered to a Soft Consistency."

"Then you . . . you *are* the Kumkwat Haagendasz . . . ?" Jazzica hissed.

"I am," he said.

Then she hesitated. "I mean, really."

"Yes, really."

Still she hesitated. "I mean, really really."

"I am, Mother."

"But c'n you be sure—?"

"There can be no doubt," Pall said firmly. "I am the One. I am It."

"Pardon me, Mauve'Bib," Spilgard said. "But could either of you explain what exactly—"

"It's Me," Pall continued. "It cannot be doubted more any longer. Period. The End."

Jazzica's eyes gleamed with her sudden appreciation of the meaning of Pall's words. "Then—"

"Yes," he said.

"So therefore—"

"Exactly, Mother."

Her eyes widened in horror. "You cannot!" she hissed.

171

"He cannot what, Revved-Up Mother?" Spilgard asked.

"Pall, you must not!" Jazzica shrilled. "What has happened to you? How can you be this way?"

"I am what you made me," he replied sharply.

"But d'you realize what you're saying?"

"What *is* he saying . . . ?" Spilgard implored nobly.

"I say what I must say," Pall stated. "Am I not your creation?"

"But—"

"Now be silent!"

"No!" Jazzica cried.

"Yes! It is done!"

"What?" Spilgard cried. "What is done?"

Jazzica felt a sudden fatigue, as though the burdens of a lifetime were lifted from her shoulders. She leaned against a wall and sighed. Pall, too, sighed, and there followed a stillness in which both of them, mother and son, radiated awe and reverence for whatever was going on.

Then Spilgard spoke.

"Mauve'Bib," he said with tentativeness in his voice through which he talked. "This Kumkwat Haagendasz of which you speak . . . what is it?"

"It is a Boni Maroni thing," Pall said.

"Yes, I was able to figure that out," the nabe said, then scratched his head, asked, "But what is it you are supposed to be? What thing may you do, as the Kumkwat Haagendasz?"

Pall looked at his mother. She met his gaze, then faltered and looked away. He turned to Spilgard.

"I am the unknown of the Boni Maroni experi-

172

ments," he said. "I am the x-factor for which they have been searching for a hundred generations."

"Yes," Spilgard nodded, frowning, then shook his head, said, "And . . . ?"

"And . . . uh . . . I . . . look, Spilgard: there are two forces in all human beings—the yes-force, and the no-force. I am He Who . . . um . . . Knows This."

Spilgard made a face of purest puzzlement, said, "But you have now told me. Does that make me a Kumkwat Haagendasz too?"

"No," Pall said, then broke away and walked toward the hall. "But come, we must assemble for council. There is not much time. I want a quantity of cocktail mix crushed and mixed with nugget-oil according to my specifications. We must assemble ingredients for a massive raid. The Emperor and the Guild alike await in space, anticipating our downfall. They think to use the Baron to defeat me, after which they will expel him on some pretext and rule Arruckus themselves, guaranteeing a supply of beer forever—which they will control. Therefore we must act swiftly. A Turbinado is gathering—a storm the size of which none of us has ever seen. It will serve our purposes handsomely."

And Pall-Mauve'Bib strode from the room out into the hootch, as Spilgard and the Lady Jazzica followed, stunned. Spilgard touched the arm of the Revved-Up Mother to stay her progress a moment, and in a voice tremulous with wonder asked, "He is able to know all this from eating peanut butter?"

She nodded, and walked swiftly after her son.

"You're probably wondering why this day I've called you all here."

They were in the central meeting hall at Hootch Grabr. Barely a day had passed since Pall had eaten of the cocktail mix, and in that span of time an army of Freedmenmen had been assembled from every major hootch in the Great Blab. Now they stood, some five million strong, and as one man attended with raptness of concentration their leader, the one they called Mauve'Bib.

"It is known to me that many of you are eager for action," Pall said. "You wish to confront the Hard-chargin filth and bake him off the face of Arruckus for all time."

"Enough talk!" cried one voice. "Let us take our flour sifters and go!"

"Aye," called another. "Even as we debate, the butter melts, the milk sours, the brown sugar gets all caked and hard!"

There came a roar of approbation. Spilgard stepped forward on the platform-ledge that faced the enormous throng, and held up his hands for silence. "Silence!" he cried. "Hear the word of Pall-Mauve'Bib!"

"Whence Spilgard's authority now?" challenged a

174

young Freedmenmen warrior. "How rules Spilgard, when the Laserium al-Dilah' is come to lead us?"

A volley of agreement voiced from the crowd, and Pall saw the fire of fanaticism in their eyes. *I must be deft here,* he thought. *Else all is lost, and my ass were as grass.*

"Freedmenmen!" Pall cried. "What would you have me do with Spilgard?"

"Fire him!" came the massed-voice reply.

The nabe, standing beside Pall, turned to him, said softly, "You cannot fire me, Mauve'Bib. I quit."

"I am prepared to accept your resignation, Spilgard," Pall said in a commanding tone, that the assembled might hear. "But know that, if you quit, I shall tender my own resignation effective immediately."

"You . . . you cannot," Spilgard gasped.

"I can, and shall."

"Mauve'Bib is Boss!" cried a voice from the floor. "He can never be fired, nor can he quit!"

Pall turned to the crowd. "Freedmenmen!" he called. "Would you deny me the use of my right arm? Would you forbid me the service of a gal friday? Would you ask me to cook with but one spoon? Would you? Could you?"

"No!" they responded.

"Then," he said, "why do you ask me to can Spilgard the nabe?"

There paused a quiet. Then shouted one man, "It is the way!" A general murmur of agreement rumbled.

"Ways change," Pall said.

"That's true!" cried a young man.

"Some ways don't change!" pointed out another voice.

"That's also true!" agreed a person.

"Enough!" Pall ordered. "What do we want in a leader? We want judgment, talent, intelligence, an ability to work with others, and that certain creative something I call the Z-factor. Has not Spilgard these qualities in abundance?"

"Yes," many answered.

"Then it is settled!" Pall said. "Spilgard remains!"

"Yes!"

Pall turned to Spilgard. "That is, if you'll stay, Spil."

The nabe worked his chin with a gnarled hand, thinking. "Well . . . I'll stay—but not as nabe. To remain thus, yet take orders from you—it would look bad, Mauve'Bib."

"I understand," Pall said. "Here, then: we shall amend your title to Nabe Emeritus and Adviser to the Messiah. We'll make of it a consultancy thing."

Spilgard spoke with the dignity of a Freedmenmen who, when he sees a good thing, knows it. "That will be satisfactory."

"Good." Pall turned to the crowd, cried, "Spilgard accepts!"

There was an outcry of approval, and the roar of five million warriors resounded throughout the cavern. As Pall surveyed the frenzied mob, a messenger approached.

"Mauve'Bib, I come from the forward observation stations," he said. "The Turbinado gathers, and the Emperor's 'Ighliner has landed at Arrucksack. The

Baron is there now, with Filp-Rotha. They make ready for the bakeoff."

"With the Guild and NOAMCHOMSKI waiting patiently in the wings, no doubt," Pall said. "Spil, the hour is come. Send out teams of brewworkers for nuts. Have pretzelmen stand by with every lumper they can muster. Tell the various nabes to take their men to the assigned places."

"At once, Mauve'Bib." Spilgard strode off to see to the arrangements.

"Freedmenmen!" Pall cried. There came a depthless silence like none had ever known among the tribes of Arruckus. "Are you ready to bake?"

As one voice they roared reply. "Yes!"

"Then let's bake!"

And as a single massive multi-form five-million-bodied creature they swarmed from the cavern.

Yes, we'll bake, Pall thought with grim determination. *And we'll do oh, so much more . . .*

And there came the time when all eyes in the known universe did turn and look toward Arruckus, metaphorically speaking.

—from "'Look Out, Space-Time Continuum! Here We Come!': The Freedmenmen Story," by the Princess Serutan

The Baron Vladimir Hardchargin stood before His Imperial Majesty, the Pahdedbrah Emperor Shaddap IV, with emotions mixed, if mastered. His vast fatgirth required both suspension and detention beams, fixed

177

about his belt. On these he now floated, glancing nervously about the night club room he had taken such pains to decorate.

They were in the main performing lounge of the Shadvlad Rendezvous, a cabaret called the Superstar Room. The club had long since been cleared of its intergalactic customers. Grim Hardehaurhar bouncers now stood guard at the doors, beside curt signs reading PRIVATE PARTY.

The Baron had spent days in this room, fretting over fabrics and lamp placements. Yet even the sight of his creative endeavors failed to give comfort. Glancing at a broad run of banquette along a wall, he flushed red with abrupt rage.

Jonzun Fillup will pay for his negligence, he thought. *Why didn't he tell me black velvet attracts so much lint?*

The Emperor cleared his throat, passed across the Baron a dismissive glance. The chair upon which he sat, centered upon the stage, was none other than the great Crystal Vanishing Throne created by his forebear, Shaddap I. It was a massive thing, hewn from a single transparent block of Hegel quartz, shot through with self-transcending bits of dialectical material. The Emperor himself was slim, weathered-looking, clad in a jumpsuit of his family colors, black on black. An armorial crest could be seen on his left breast pocket, the image of an invisible man.

The Baron glanced to the side of the Emperor and was discomfited to see an old woman in a black robe, her skin wrinkled, her single good eye a milky white, her nose a carrot. This was the Revved-Up Mother George Cynthia Mohairem, an elder of the Boni

178

Maroni order and the Emperor's personal Truth Consequencer. The Baron stifled a shudder. The witch's presence could bode naught but ill.

As for the rest of the retinue, there were the usual attendants and servants, with two exceptions. A pair of Schlepping Guildsmen stood nearby. One was heavy with brawn, the other lean and stringy, yet both had the dark glasses and pot-belly of their kind. It was unclear to the Baron what their interest was in these proceedings, although it almost certainly concerned the beer.

To the side the Baron could see his nephew, Filp-Rotha, standing in edgy obeisance but obvious in his restlessness. He seemed to be eyeing someone in the Imperial party; the Baron's heart stopped beating when he followed his nephew's insolent gaze.

The little fool! the Baron thought. *He eyegives to the Emperor's daughter!*

It was Serutan, Shaddap's eldest, a tall, blonde young woman clad in the flowing white apron of the Boni Maroni novice. Her name, the Baron knew, was "natures" spelled backwards. But, whether this was some sort of arcane public relations move on Shaddap's part, or merely a fluke of the child-naming, the Baron could not say. House Hardchargin was not skilled at bestowing upon children names that exposed meaning when read backwards. "Filp-Rotha," when reversed, was "Ahtor-Plif"—a word which the Baron was forced to concede served no apparent utility.

"So, Baron," the Emperor said. "Or should I call you 'Partner'?"

"As you please, Majesty," the Baron said. "I welcome you to the bakeoff, and feel confident—"

179

"The bakeoff!" cackled the old woman, rubbing her bony hands together.

"Yes," the Baron said anxiously. "I have summoned the one they call Mauve'Bib, and expect his arrival shortly."

"I am told there is a sugar storm building," the Emperor said. "A full-fledged Turbinado. Surely you do not think even this fanatic Mauve'Bib will travel here under such conditions."

"He is mad, Majesty. They all are. I fully expect—"

"You expect," the Emperor replied dryly. "You speak much of your expectations, Baron—"

"Expectations!" the Revved-Up Mother wheezed with glee. "Speak much!"

"Yet," the Emperor said with a certain Revved-Up-Mother-directed asperity, "your expectations have a way of not being met."

"Majesty . . . ? I don't . . ." the Baron gulped. "I'm not sure what you mean . . ."

"Oh, come, now, Baron," replied Shaddap. "Surely—"

"Come now!" hissed the Truth Consequencer. "Surely!"

"Please, Your Extremely Revved-Uppedness," the Emperor said with forced smile. "May I?" He turned to the Baron. "We were speaking of your expectations. You told me you expected this establishment to be refurbished and decorated in six months. In fact it took thirteen."

"That was Jonzun Fillup's fault, Majesty!" the Baron cried. "The man's a narcissistic popinjay! Spends all his time attending social functions!"

180

"And yet you spoke so highly of him before," the Emperor observed. "How odd . . . Well, no matter. But you assured me you expected to have the pretzels under control in less than a year. I arrive to discover they are as rampant as ever."

"Rampant!" cackled the old woman. "I arrive! They are!"

"They're very big, Majesty—"

"Indeed. And you promised me you expected to have the Freedmenmen out of business by now. Yet I am told they flourish." The Emperor's eyes flashed fury. "Customers throng the lobbies waiting for *their* coffee cake vendors, while our Aldebaran pastry chefoids watch helpless beside dessert carts groaning under full weight!"

"They have become much more skillful over the past year, Majesty," the Baron stuttered. "They use recipes hitherto known only to Boni Maroni adepts."

"Indeed?" the Emperor murmured, and turned to glance at the Revved-Up Mother George Cynthia Mohairem.

The old woman scowled and nodded. "Their use of pine nuts," she muttered. "Dead giveaway. Old Boni Maroni trick. We *invented* pine nuts—!"

"All shall be remedied today, Majesty," the Baron said firmly. "Once we defeat this Mauve'Bib, they'll fall quickly into line. Besides," he added, feeling a rising hope. "How many of them can there be? A handful of villages, each with a population of a few thousand at most? We . . . that is, you . . . can bounce them from here to Updike Centauri."

"You think them no match for my Hardehaurhar,

181

eh?" the Emperor asked. "You think my bouncers may dispatch them to wherever they please . . . ?"

"Well, Majesty, it is said—"

"Silence." The Emperor turned to address the two Guildsmen. "Gentlemen, you requested to be present at this meeting to deliver a message to the Baron here. Now is your chance."

"Eh?" the Baron squawked, turning on his suspensors to face them.

The Guildsmen stepped forward with the pot-bellied swagger typical of their kind. *Why do they all wear those damned sunglasses?* the Baron wondered.

The tall thin one spoke, addressing the Baron. "You got a problem, good buddy," he drawled.

"Wh—?"

"We don't care what kind of Canopan six-legged gazelle piss you serve in this here club," he said. "But you been sending us the same thing, and that just don't seem right, now, do it?"

The Baron turned haplessly to the Emperor. "Majesty," he croaked, "what are they talking about . . . ?"

"Ya waterin' downa beeah," snarled the heavyset Guildsman.

The Baron's face drained white. He choked, then stammered, "*I?*"

"You's da head man heah, aintcha?" the beefy one queried.

"Well, but—"

"The Guild is perturbed, Baron," the Emperor purred. "They believe you to be diluting their supplies of beer and pocketing the profits yourself. Thus far I have been able to stay their wrath. I need hardly

182

remind you how important beer is to a Guildsman . . ."

"We got the whole membership on a conference-call interlink," the lean Guildsman said. " 'less we get a convincin' assurance from you and Shaddap here, we're gonna call ourselves a general strike an' shut 'er down across the whole known damn universe." He spat without emotion on the floor at the Baron's feet. "No brew, no deliv'ries."

"Of . . . anything?"

The thin Guildsman spat again, stared the Baron in the eye, drawled, "That's a great big affirmatory, good buddy."

The Baron backed off from the two Guildsmen in a frantic swirl of robes and flashing suspensors. "Majesty, it wasn't me," he gasped. "I swear it! Why would I risk offending the Guild? I need their deliveries for food, for linen—for everything!"

"We all do, Baron," the Emperor said with chilling quiet. "A general strike by the Guild would cripple NOAMCHOMSKI, and could put us all out of business. Have you any idea how the Great Big Houses would react to a member who brought about such a calamity? Death would seem a mercy."

"I know!" the Baron gulped. "That's why I would never—"

"These gentlemen have agreed to hold off the rank and file for a few days while you convince them of your innocence," the Emperor said. "And to give you time to rectify the situation."

"I . . . I will," the Baron gasped. "Once the bakeoff is completed—"

There was a flurry among the assembled courts-people, and their ranks were split by the hastening arrival of a doorman. He scurried up to the edge of the stage and bowed before the Emperor. "Majesty, someone is at the door—"

"We're closed," the Emperor said irritably. "Comp them some drinks in the Starlight—"

"Peel, seed, and dice one medium-sized cucumber," said a clear young voice.

All heads turned to see a young girl-child, having barely two years of aging in her chronological duration of lifespan, clad in a Freedmenmen sweatsuit of playful bright yellow. She walked with bold simplicity into the night club.

"Here, now, who is this?" the Emperor asked.

"That recipe!" the Revved-Up Mother whispered. "It is familiar to me . . ."

The Emperor leaned over and addressed the female-pre-schooler-person. "Tell me, dear, who sent you here?"

The girl said, "Blend the spices, vinegar, and sugar in an Ixmaster. Pour this mixture over the cucumber."

The Revved-Up Mother stepped forward and with a look of horror pointed a gnarled finger at the girl. "It is a Boni Maroni recipe! For Sliced Rigelian Yak-Birds in Anti-Fish Sauce! She cannot know it!"

"Indeed," the Emperor mused. "Nor can she possibly know that the machinists on Ix-Nay have at last perfected a practical blender." He looked at the girl. "Child—"

"She is an abomination!" the Boni Maroni elder cried.

184

The child held up her hand. In it was a single folded sheet of beerpaper, Shaddap took it and perused its contents. "'I am Nailya, daughter of Duke Lotto Agamemnides and the Lady Jazzica, and sister of Pall-Mauve'Bib,'" he read aloud. "'I bring greetings from my brother to the Emperor Shaddap IV, and invite him to witness the bakeoff, which shall commence momentarily.'"

"You see, Majesty?" the Baron squealed. "He's coming in spite of the storm! They are mad!"

"Perhaps," the Emperor said, rising from his chair. "Or perhaps they are clever. The storm traps me here in Arrucksack. This they know. It appears this Mauve'Bib is particularly eager that I attend the bakeoff. Why? Unless he—"

He could not finish. A sudden roar grew around the building, and a panic arose among the gathered courtiers. "It is only the storm!" the Emperor called. He had to shout above the rising, whining din of the ever-mounting Turbinado. "Baron, do you still believe this Mauve'Bib will come? In a gale like this? Tell me, are there windows in here?"

"Uh, no, Majesty," the Baron stammered. "My scheme called—I mean, Jonzun Fillup's scheme called for eliminating them in the cabaret. I fought the man tooth and nail, of course, but—"

"Spare me this latest lie, Baron, and take me to windows. Immediately."

The Baron gathered his senses and commanded aides to conduct him and the Emperor out into the lobby. Swiftly the Imperial party swept from the cabaret, the court trailing. The Baron followed.

185

This Emperor arrives surrounded by fops and fawners, lackeys and layabouts, hangers-on and sycophants of the most useless and contemptible sort, the Baron thought disgustedly as he floated out of the cabaret. *Some men have all the luck.*

They came to the lobby, a long curving space walled on one side by a vast red curtain. "Open," the Emperor commanded.

An aide drew aside the huge expanses of velvet, exposing large picture windows that looked out onto the plains beyond the city.

And for the first time in his life, the Pahdedbrah Emperor, Shaddap IV, found himself speechless with amazement.

Below, covering an area of hundreds of square kilometers, came a wave-upon-wave phalanx of giant pretzels. They swept through the swirling, raging sugar storm in a relentless assault, spewing up tons of sugar into the already-murky air as they plowed through the dark brown hardpack toward the city.

Yet what utterly confounded the Emperor was what, even at that height and distance, he was able to discern upon the backs of the giant snack-beasts: hundreds, thousands, possibly millions of Freedmenmen, their sweatshirt hoods up and tied, riding in well-ordered ranks upon the very bodies of the immense creatures.

"B-b-but . . . the Shield," the Baron stuttered. "How did they get past the Shield? It was electronically tested in our special machines . . ."

"It leaked," sneered Filp-Rotha, standing nearby. "Obviously."

186

"My apologies, Baron," the Emperor said crisply. "It seems there will indeed be a bakeoff today." He turned to the Hardehaurhar Commander. "Captain, assemble your people at the front door. I want those madmen denied entrance. Do whatever you have to—invoke ad hoc Dress Code. Require jackets and ties."

"But Your Majesty . . . for lunch?"

"Anything. Just keep them out. Then bring Mauve 'Bib to me."

There came a great crashing at the entrance to the city. Two Hardehaurhar burst into the lobby. "They've breached the gate!" one cried. "Majesty, to the back office!"

The Emperor looked at the Baron with a dark scowl. "You're finished in this business, Hardchargin," he said, then, surrounded by Hardehaurhar, made his way up an escalator for the master offices.

Meanwhile, thousands of the terrorist bouncer–fanatics swarmed through the building as, in endless flood, hosts of Freedmenmen swept into the Shadvlad Rendezvous. And it was hand to hand pushing and shoving in the largest and most luxurious cocktail lounge in the known universe, as House Hardehaurhar was confronted with a party of five million that would be admitted with or without a reservation, regardless of dress code.

Above, in the master office, the Emperor scowled at television monitor screens. Their message was unambiguous. He turned to the Revved-Up Mother George Cynthia Mohairem and indicated, on the screen, a group of Freedmenmen.

"What are those jars they carry?" he asked. "Of that brownish paste?"

She shook her head, looked grave. "I can but guess, Majesty," she said. "The color resembles one thing native to this accursed planet."

"And that is . . . ?"

She screwed her aged face in contempt and not a little awe.

"Peanuts," she said.

He was chef and slob, customer and cashier, lunatic and assistant electrician, warrior and shortstop. He was a saint, yet he was a man. He was a highly respected leader, yet he was also a great disappointment. He was not content until his people were free, yet he would not be truly happy until he had made his mother miserable. He strode across Arruckus like he owned the place. Who did he think he was? If he's so ineffable, let him write his own damn biography.

—from "No More Princess Nice Guy: The Princess
Serutan Story," by the Princess Serutan

It was to the Superstar Cabaret Room that they brought Pall-Mauve'Bib on the afternoon of his victory. The bakeoff itself they had conducted in the Imperial Room, largest of the bars with hot hors d'oeuvre capability. There had Pall supervised the creation of a number of special dishes—satays, cookies, soups—that made strategic use of the peanut butter he had created from the cocktail mix, the salt-dried remnants of the giant pretzels.

The chefs of the Baron Hardchargin had been no match for the young man, whose tasty, exotic, yet surprisingly do-able recipes had been transmitted orally to him by his sister, Nailya the Truly Weird. She had received them from her ancestors, eons-dead, while still in her mother's womb. The dramatic presentation of each new dish had brought gasps of sudden recognition from the Revved-Up Mother George Cynthia Mohairem, to whom they were but dimly known from Boni Maroni texts, index cards, and old newspaper columns.

During the competition the old woman found a moment to confer with the Lady Jazzica. She turned an accusing eye on the younger woman, said, "You've betrayed secrets we of the Boni Maroni've held for generations, Jazzica. I'll have you blackballed."

"I've betrayed nothing," Jazzica replied. "Besides, would you blackball the woman who's given birth to the Kumkwat Haagendasz?"

The crone darted a suspicious glance, hissed, "You mean—?"

"Yes."

The hag gasped with sudden comprehension. "Then—"

"Exactly."

"So therefore—"

"In all probability."

"And—"

"It is inevitable."

It had gone on like this for half an hour, the two women communicating via suggestions and shrugs, leading questions not completed and hinted answers not begun, secret Boni Maroni hand signals, sign language, eye blinks, and charades. By the end Jazzica knew a certain thing: she hadn't the slightest idea what had been discussed.

But neither does she, she thought with satisfaction.

Now they again faced each other, this time across the vast tabled-and-chaired floor of the cabaret lounge. Jazzica noted the old woman clung close to the Emperor and his retinue, and wondered how the Revved-Up Mother'd be treated under the terms Pall would propose for their resumption of the family business.

And what of the Emperor himself? she mused.

She decided Pall'd probably keep Shaddap around as a greeter, one of those informal host-positions by which retired athletes and deposed royalty earned a few solaris rubbing elbows with conventioneers and posing for egolikeness laserpix with tourists.

Yet a glance at her son revealed little of his purpose.

Pall sat on a chair set on the stage, the Emperor's throne having been carted off to the wings. Jazzica and Spilgard flanked him, with the Feydeaukin humor commandoes arrayed around the periphery.

Now is the ripeness of time in the most delicate of balance, thought Pall, gazing across the room at the vanquished who filed in before him. *Now let the fate of my life be sealed, that I may bring to fruition every secret hope and aspiration which, being realized, will alter forever everything, and make me rich and famous.*

Pall motioned to Spilgard. "Have the Baron step forward," he said.

190

"At once, Mauve'Bib."

He obeys me like a god, no longer like a comrade, Pall thought. *He's learning.*

"So, my Lord Baron," Pall said. "At last we meet face to face."

The fat man quivered in his suspensors as he floated toward the stage. "You've won," he said nervously. "I see that. It's deserved, no doubt about it. Those chocolate–peanut butter brownies were superb. Superb!"

"I'm glad you liked them."

"Liked? Loved! Adored! But . . ." The man's face went pale, his manner faltered. "What are you going to do now? With me, I mean?"

"You ruined my father," Pall said. "You seized our property, sent us into exile and a life of fear and deprivation. You proved yourself inept in the management of this club, vulgar in taste as a decorator and designer, and clumsy in public relations. What do you think I should do with you?"

The man hesitated, then in a small voice said timorous, "Kick me upstairs?"

Pall waved a hand dismissively, said to his guards, "He's fired. Get him out of my sight."

"What?" the Baron cried, looking wildly about. "No! You can't! I've got friends! I've got connections! I've got a contract!"

"It's trash," Pall said. "Your deal is with the Emperor. My victory renders it null and void."

The Baron spied, standing nearby, the two Guildsmen. It was to them that he drifted frantically over,

191

pudgy hands upraised imploringly. "Help me!" he cried. "We've always done business! Say something—he'll listen to you!"

The lean, stringy Guildsman looked back impassively, his sunglasses making of his eyes two unreadable black disks. "I don't think my constituency'd cotton t'me helping out a fella who waters down beer," he said with pan dead. "Good buddy."

"But it wasn't me!" the Baron cried. "It was him!" He whirled and pointed toward Pall. "Him and those Freedmenmen scum! They did it!"

"Sorry, Bar'n," the Guildsman said. "You're out."

"Why, you—"

In a single hysterical motion the Baron lashed out, slapped the Guildsman. Gasps audibled throughout the cabaret. Guards rushed forward, seized the fat man. Then they, too, gasped, as they beheld the stoic unflinchingness of the tall, lanky Guildsman.

The blow had jarred loose his sunglasses, revealing his eyes underneath. They stared out an undifferentiated red-on-red, the deepest unfathomable crimsons of the beer-addicted. Unhurriedly, the Guildsman bent down, retrieved the glasses, and put them back on. He looked out wordlessly once again from the all-but-opaque dark disks.

Pall observed this without reaction. *I knew it,* he thought. *Those guys drink more beer than anybody. The Guild is mine.*

He motioned to his aides, indicated the weeping Baron, commanded, "Remove him."

The Baron turned, raged, "I'll sue!"

"See you in court."

"Hold!"

All looked toward the rear of the room. A young man made his way through the crowd. The Baron glanced sharply up, face suffused with relief, gasped, "Filp!"

And Filp-Rotha strode up to the stage upon which sat Pall-Mauve'Bib. He said in a clear firm voice, "So this is the Mauve'Bib who leads this pathetic gang of sugar-rats, eh? None other than Pall Agamemnides."

"Ah-h-h-h, Filp-Rotha," Pall murmured. "I've been expecting you."

"Correct me if I'm wrong, Agamemnides," Filp-Rotha sneered, "But I'm under the impression that your mother's like a streetcar—twenty-five cents to get on."

A gasp hissed through the chamber. Pall, smiling, said, "Do you call me out? Is this rankout challenge?"

"It is," Filp-Rotha said. "I will rank you out in ten minutes, and have this place reopened for Happy Hour."

Pall stood and motioned toward the stage. "Then come up. Ladies and gentlemen, a hand for a young talent—Filp-Rotha Hardchargin."

Does Pall know what he's doing? Jazzica thought in fear. *This youth is no mere amateur . . . !*

Applause smattered as Filp-Rotha leaped onto the stage. Pall rose, allowed aides to remove his chair. Now the platform was clear, save for the chairs and music stands in the rear for the band. Filp-Rotha grabbed a standup microphone, flung it contemptuously aside.

193

"I don't think we need this," he said. "My rankout is audible to the deaf old lady in the back row."

He's overconfident, Pall thought. *That'll help.*

Filp-Rotha assumed rankout stance stage right, as Pall positioned himself stage left. Jazzica could sense a tensioning in the audience. Pall's Feydeaukin body-guards began to edge forward. *They'll never permit this to go through,* she thought. *They'll shout the Hard-chargin boy down before he can score a hit.*

"Come, Agamemnides," Filp-Rotha said with curling lip. "You start. Make me cringe with the ferocity of your insult."

"After you," Pall said quietly. "This is my club now. Visiting team always goes first."

Filp-Rotha's eyes narrowed. "Your club? Hah! Very well, Freedmenmen brat—" He took a breath, feigned a smile, then quickly said, "You make me—"

A chaos arose from the floor as six Feydeaukin warriors raced in and out of the room, slamming doors and crying, "B-way b.o. boffo! B-way b.o. boffo!"

"Hold!" Pall commanded. "Feydeaukin, stay! Let this proceed."

"But why, beloved?" cried a voice.

Pall searched the crowd, found the source of the question.

Loni!

"Mauve'Bib need not do this thing," the child-woman said.

"But Pall Agamemnides must, Babycakes," Pall replied. "It is a p.r. thing."

"We can remove this insect in a moment,

194

Mauve'Bib," said another voice. Pall recognized the sober tones of Spilgard.

"I know, Spil," Pall said. "But it is something I must do."

Pall saw the nabe shrug. "So be it," Spilgard said.

"Finished consulting with your women and Freedmenmen friends, Agamemnides?" Filp-Rotha taunted. "Or perhaps you'd like to ask advice from the busboys as well?"

"Finished," Pall replied. "Let us begin."

The two resumed their stance across the stage from one another. The room was now utterly silent. Pall studied his opponent's face—Filp-Rotha appeared to be working himself up into a scathing fury. He said nothing for an endless two minutes, instead pacing in small steps back and forth, eyes narrowed at Pall, mouth working silently.

Suddenly he struck. "If I had a face like yours, Agamemnides, I'd shave my—"

Pall stepped forward.

Now! he thought.

With a whipsnap motion he reached into the side pocket of his sweatshirt and produced his swysknife. And in a single sweep of arm-wrist-hand, he unfolded the largest of its blades and flung the thing toward Filp-Rotha. It landed home at his heart, stuck there.

"—and walk backwards." Filp-Rotha was able to complete his rankout before falling heavily to the stage, lifeless.

The silence was of sufficient thickness it could be thinly sliced.

195

Pall faced the stunned crowd, announced, "Now let the Emperor and his Truth Consequencer come forth."

As an unthinking thing the crowd parted, granting walk-through to the Pahdedbrah Emperor, Shaddap IV, and the Revved-Up Mother George Cynthia Mohairem. The Emperor, tall and slim in his black jumpsuit, walked erect, with regal calm. The old woman, in her black cloak, skulked furtive and sneaky, staying close by his side.

"And will you kill me, too?" the Emperor said in a clear voice.

"If necessary," Pall replied. "But I think you will accede to my terms, rendering that option superfluous."

"Why should I believe you?" the Emperor demanded. "You violated the rules of rankout by plunging a knife into that boy's heart. How can you expect anyone to do business with you after such treachery?"

"I am no longer in business," Pall said.

"Pall!" Jazzica gasped. "D'you realize what you're saying—?"

"I do, Mother." Pall looked at the Emperor. "I'm no longer in business," he repeated. "I'm in control."

"Very impressive," the Emperor said. "And how d'you propose to remain in control? D'you honestly suppose the Great Big Houses will permit—"

"The Great Big Houses will do what I tell them," Pall said evenly. "They will do anything so long as their business interests are protected."

"Then your terms include—"

"These are my terms," Pall said. "The hand of your

196

daughter in marriage, with your entire holdings in NOAMCHOMSKI as dowry. Plus a complete eight-piece sterling silver dinner service for ten in a pattern of our choosing."

"Sterling? You are indeed mad!"

Pall regarded the Emperor, said with exquisite care, "Very well. Forget the silverware. I shall be too busy to entertain, anyway. I intend to use all the NOAM-CHOMSKI profits to convert Arruckus into what it should be, and should always have been—a planet-sized theme restaurant. Further, I—"

"Pardon me, Mauve'Bib." Spilgard stepped forward, said gently, "But what about our dream of entrees? Of a new Doon, where we Freedmenmen and our children may enjoy a halfway balanced diet after four centuries of persecution, rejection, and bad teeth?"

"There will be entrees, Spil. This I promise," Pall said. "But we'll have to import them. We can't grow cow one out on those sugars."

"And our children, and their children . . . ?"

"They'll all work in the restaurant," Pall said, and held up his right hand in solemn oath. "This thing I swear: they'll eat the same meals as any patron. Anything they want on the menu. With certain seasonal exceptions, of course."

He must caution! Jazzica thought. *Else he'll give away the store in benefits and perks!*

"You demand my daughter and NOAMCHOMSKI," the Emperor said with sarcasm. "And I suppose I—"

"You and your court shall be exiled to Salacia Simplicissimus, where you will open for Oyeah, the

197

false accountant," Pall said. "You will command a troop of trained Arcturan dogs, which you will teach to play a selected medley of show songs on a rack of tuned bicycle horns."

"Guildsmen!" the Emperor called. "Do you hear this lunatic? Join me, and together we shall restore order to the universe!"

"They will not, Majesty," Pall said. "For they know that, should they defy me, I shall command my Freedmenmen to summon every pretzel on this planet, and to destroy them."

The Emperor laughed raucous hearty. "You'd be doing us a favor!" he said. "I've been after Hardchargin to eliminate those things for years!"

"It were better for you he was unable to do so," Pall said. "Were the pretzels to die, all source of beer on Arruckus would disappear. Within a year this world would be utterly and eternally dry." He indicated the two Guildsmen. "Ask them. They know."

The Emperor whirled. "Is this true?" he demanded.

The lean Guildsman spat on the floor, eyed the Emperor, said, "Yep."

The Emperor turned back to Pall. "And if I refuse? If I swear a vow of kramden and send my entire staff of Hardehaurhar against you?"

"Then I will kill you."

The Emperor blanched and seemed to rock backward. "Kill?" he said slowly, then, "But that's against the law . . ."

"For others of the race, yes," Pall said. "But one of my superior abilities is bound by a higher law. Depend on it, Majesty. I will kill you."

Raising his voice, Pall declared to the assembled crowd, "Just as I will kill anyone else who gainsays my will. I need listen to no man now. For I am the Kumkwat Haagendasz, and what I say, it goes."

"Brave words," the Emperor said, but there were inflection-tones of being-afraid in his voice-speaking. "What power have you to back them up?"

"I have the Boni Maroni, for one," Pall said. "They will support me because I offer them something even you cannot." He shot a glance at the Revved-Up Mother George Cynthia Mohairem, whispered, "New ingredients!"

The old woman's eye narrowed. "Name two," she croaked.

"The peanut butter you did sample this day," Pall replied. "And a thing even more precious—the beer liqueur."

"Then it's so!" she gasped. "The rumors—"

"—are purest truth," Pall said. "The liqueur is perfected. You shall be receiving samples of it in about a week, together with a money-saving coupon."

"Pall," said a voice. All eyes turned toward the Lady Jazzica. "Would you dispense samples of a thing that still lacks a name?"

"It has a name, Mother," Pall said. "A name that did come to me that night in the Brewer Room." He paused cornily dramatic, said, "I call it: Drambrewski."

"Enough!" snarled the Emperor. "You may purchase the support of a cooking school full of women, Agamemnides. But do you truly think to defeat me, and the combined might of the Great

199

Big Houses, with peanut butter and after-dinner drinks?"

Pall smiled. "I have, for that, a strength unequalled in all the universe," he said. "I have my people."

He looked beyond the Emperor, toward the five million assembled warriors. "Freedmenmen! Will you not obey the word of Mauve'Bib without hesitation? Are not his enemies yours? Is he not the Boss of Bosses?"

And there arose a mighty cheer from the Freedmenmen, from all save Spilgard, whose aspect reflected a worried concern at the possible loss of the tribes' democratic tradition.

Pall turned back to the Emperor. "They are my muscle, my sinew, my torpedoes and my soldiers. No force known to man can stop them. And I intend to lead them on a mission throughout the universe, to cleanse and purify civilization itself. I am the Kumkwat Haagendasz, and the Kumkwat Haagendasz is me. That is all you need know. Ask for me by name."

Pall motioned to a guard and indicated the Emperor. "Take him and his Boni Maroni hag away."

Jazzica approached Pall and looked deeply into his eyes. Their red-on-red met hers. "My son," she said, and spoke with difficulty. "Before, I had doubts as to the wisdom of your path. I thought you wild with the recklessness of youth, and I cursed the impulse that had led me to give you birth. Yet I have this day experienced a change of heart. For there are indeed more important things than regaining the family business, and one of these is ruling the universe. You are the

200

superior product of the race, and your rule'll last a thousand years. It's the fitting culmination of your training."

"Thanks, Mother," Pall said. "And for yourself, what would you have?"

"I?" Jazzica thought, then smiled. "Why, I hardly know. A few planets. An army of slaves. Perhaps a new apartment. I shall need time to decide."

"You shall have that time. And I shall have—this woman."

Pall held out his hand to a tall blonde woman who had lingered on the outskirts of the Imperial party.

She stepped forward, chin held high. Her father, the Emperor, stayed her with an outstretched hand.

"Is this what you want, Daughter?" he asked.

"Yes, Father," she said simply. "It is what I have been trained for. My life-choices are few, the options straightforward. I may wear a sequined bathing suit on a prison planet, and assist you with a dog act opening for a bad comedian. Or I may be wife to the ruler of the universe." She looked downward in shy obeisance, said with becoming modesty and respect, "I have made my decision."

Pall scanned the crowd, found Loni in lip-trembling shakiness. "Do not worry, Beloved," he said to her. "I like you, too."

Then Pall-Mauve'Bib held up his hands and proclaimed, "Come, Freedmenmen! The universe is rank with decadence and corruption! It is given to us this day to do battle with the Great Satan of depravity that holds sway on every planet in the Imperium! Will you

201

follow me on a holy crusade, to lay low the wicked in My Name?"

And there arose a Sound in that cabaret such as had never before been heard in the known Universe. It was the noise of five million Freedmenmen voices raised as one, in a single reverberating cry of "Aw-w-w-w re-e-e-e-t!"

Then confusion pandemoniumed, as the Freed-menmen exploded from the room and flooded throughout the Shadvlad Rendezvous. They carried the one they called Mauve'Bib upon their shoulders, in triumph both culinary and politico-religious.

And in that chaos, Jazzica found Loni. The girl-child was dazed with the splendor and swiftness of Mauve-'Bib's ascension to power—and melancholy fearful over his choice of wife.

"Worry not, Loni," Jazzica said. "He'll not forsake you. The marriage is purely political. He chooses the daughter Serutan, who I am told has certain literary aspirations."

"Her husband will be ruler of the universe," Loni said. "She'll not have much trouble finding a publisher."

"Perhaps. But she'll be his wife in name only."

"I know, Revved-Up Mother," Loni said. "It will be strange. She, the legal wife, will know none of his caresses or tender looks, except maybe sometimes. Yet I, the concubine—history will call me wife."

"History can call you whatever it wants," Jazzica said. "As long as it doesn't call you late for dinner."

Loni looked at her. "I do not understand, Revved-Up Mother."

Jazzica sighed, thought, *This one, too, has so much to learn.*

"One day you will, my dear," she said. "One day you will."

APPENDIX

In studying the Imperium and Arruckus, many unfamiliar terms are failed to be understood. To comprehend is praiseworthy as a thing, hence this glossary of the following words may be read.

A

AARGH: Rocky, uneven, frustrating landscape.

ABDUL-JABBAR: "The high-handed, long-legged enemy." A small thing you can kill somebody with somehow. Used by Boni Maronites for frightening children. Also known as the "sky-hook."

AMWAY RULE: In Freedmenmen society, the right to challenge an opponent, who is thereby required either to give satisfaction, or delegate a congenial group of friends, relatives, and neighbors who may purchase franchise rights for providing satisfaction themselves.

ANTARES TELEPORT AND TELEPATH: Giant communications corporation known for the controversial design of its headquarters planet (Jonzun Fillup, arch.).

ARRUCKUS: The planet known as Doon; third planet of Canopeas.

ASSOL: A fool; someone who behaves badly.

AWW-REEET!: Freedmenmen cry of exultation. Second syllable can be drawn out for as long as the exulter opts.

BALLY-SHOES: Insanely expensive footwear, commonly worn by nobility.

BEAVER: In Freedmenmen argot, a young girl. And that's all. Just a young girl.

BEE-EFF-DEE: Derisive, sarcastic teenage slang for "So what?" or "Big deal." Derivation unknown.

BEER: (also Foam, Suds, Brewski, Frosty, etc.) The nut/yeast beverage of the wilds of Arruckus, formed by a process of snacko-catalysis and deep-sugar fermentation from the decomposed bodies of pretzels.

BEER BELLIES: Small pockets of mature beer found on the surface of Arruckus after a "beer blast."

BEER BLAST: Convulsive explosion that occurs when subterranean deposits of "brew" reach maturity.

BEERBURP: Sudden percussive release, from the stomach through the mouth, of gas ingested by drinking beer.

BEERMUG: Mug-like vessel for drinking beer-like beverages.

BEERPAPER: Paper made from beer. A Freedmenmen artifact. Nobody knows how they do it.

BEERTERRYCLOTH: Terry cloth made from beer. Not as absorbent as cotton terry cloth, but still pretty absorbent, considering.

BEERWAGON: Large vehicle used to harvest beer from the surface of Arruckus.

BENEVOLENT PLANETARY ORDER OF ELKOIDS: Interplanetary men's and male-life-forms' social organization, known for its eerie and vaguely frightening-looking meeting halls.

BIB: The traditional purple napkin worn by Freedmenmen, said to symbolize their exile from an Edenic place where they had something decent to eat.

BIG STICK: Penultimate growth stage of the giant pretzel.

BOFFO: In Varietese, Amen. (Lit., "we should be so lucky.")

BONGO WAFER: Any area of terrain on Arruckus in which sugar crystals have been fused on the molecular level, resulting in an impaction which resonates with a bongo-bop sound when struck.

BONI MARONI: Quasi-religious cooking school, established after the overthrow of the convenience and frozen food industry during the Industrial Revolution.

BOWERON: Fourth planet of Gamma Craven, known for its large population of vagrants and indigents; the "Skid Row Planet."

BRANIF: A woman whose husband, found to be teetering on the brink of moral bankruptcy, is dismissed and replaced by another.

BREW: Mixture of water, yeast, and salted peanuts that forms the "pre-beer" liquid.

BUNKY: In Freedmenmen argot, a son or young man.

C

CAL-RIPKIN SAC-FLY: Some kind of strange device used on the open sugars of Arruckus.

CALTRANS: Irregular public transportation device native to Arruckus.

CARRY-ON: Large equipment transport vehicle; also, to misbehave; also, small transport bag capable of fitting under the seat of an orthodontothopter.

C-BISCUIT: A crude, muffin-like foodstuff used by Freedmenmen for survival in the wilds.

CERTIFIED IMPERIAL ACCOUNTANT (C.I.A.): A keeper-of-books licensed by the Imperium to bookkeep.

CHAUBAKKY: Poison administered in chewing tobacco.

CHAVEZ: Poison administered in fruit.

CHIKSOOP: Dehydrated nutrient broth used by Freedmenmen in the wilds. Usually safeguarded by a krep-lock (see Krep-Lock).

CHURCH KEY: Freedmenmen religio-functional prying device used to open canisters of beer. Commonly part of a swysknife (see Swysknife).

COCKTAIL MIX: Peanut remnant of pretzel after saline decomposition. Eaten in Freedmenmen religious trance-rituals.

COOK-VOICE: A Boni Maroni technique for banishing unwanted persons from a kitchen via the implantation of a nasal, highly irritating vocal tone in their ear.

COSMOSPOLITAN: One of the primary magnetazines of the Imperium. (see Magnetazine). Specializes in topical articles encouraging women over age thirty (Standard) to pretend they're eighteen.

COWBOYDAN: Third planet of Deltoid-Pectoris; birthworld of Pall-Mauve'Bib.

D

DISCOMFORTREL: Tenacious fibrous filament made from the pish-tush vine, used for binding and gagging protagonists.

DORK: Long narrow valley, usually populated by dull, graceless people whose pants are usually too short.

E

EEK: A scary plateau or butte.

ELECTROLUX RECLINER: Form-fitting sofa that holds the body in place via vacuum suction.

ENCYCLOPEDOPHILIA PROPHYLACTICA: Multi-volume book of wisdom and knowledge, usually used by school children, concerning the importance of good hygiene when indulging in foot fetishism.

ENGLEBERTHUMPERDINCK: Proof, partic. that required to confirm a possible millenial redemption. Derivation unknown and, if known, highly implausible.

ERG: A broad plain; also, a unit of energy; also, a unit of energy expended on a broad plain.

EYE OF THE EGAD: The red-on-red eye color of deep beer addiction. Characteristic of Freedmenmen, yet also seen among offworlders, Schlepping Guildsmen, etc.

FARFEL: Slang for nonsense, bushwa, etc. Originally, little pieces of matzoh used as bulk filler.

FERNDOC: Freedmenmen device; originally, a plant physician.

FEYDEAUKIN (also Farcees): Comedy commandoes sworn to protect the person of the Mahdl-T, or die laughing. Their traditional strategy involves the intensive application of running in and out of rooms and slamming doors, thus confusing their adversary.

FILTCIG: Freedmenmen survival tool, consisting of a cigarette with a filter attached to one end.

FLAMTAP: Rudimentary Freedmenmen drum device used for communication across short distances.

FLOTZ: A song or ballad.

FOAMFALL: The subsiding of the head of a mug of beer.

FREEDMENMEN: The native tribes of Arruckus, said to be descended from the Nancee Druze peoples of the Ad Astra Diaspora.

FREEN: On Arruckus, any low-lying depression created by the subsiding of an underlying basement complex; also, any lowdown lying depressive suffering from an unresolved basement complex.

G

GETTY PREMIUM: The planet of Ofiorucci B (36), homeworld of House Hardchargin.

GNOCCHIS: Ears, so-called because of that organ's

resemblance to an ancient foodstuff formed of potato flour.

GREAT BIG HOUSES: Holders of planetary fiefs (usually an extended bloodline) who live in large single-family dwellings. Also, the dwellings themselves.

H

HAJJ-PAJJ: A mixture of many kinds of pilgrimages and sacred journeys to a jumble of different places for a variety of confused reasons.

HALF-WIFE: A wife inherited from another man after rankout combat.

HAL-PRINTZ!: "Terrific!" or "I love it!" Also may mean "Well-staged!"

HARDEHAURHAR: Terrorist bouncer-fanatics in service to the Emperor.

HEGEL QUARTZ: Ultraclear crystalline rock speckled with bits of self-transcending dialectical material.

HOKI-POKI: A ritualistic dancelike movement used to dance, or to move ritualistically.

HOOTCH: A Freedmenmen village.

I

'IGHLINER: Schlepping Guild space frigate and, by law, the largest man-made thing permitted to exist in the Imperium.

IMPERIAL INSTITUTE OF ACCOUNTING AND BROADCASTING: A fully-accredited learning institution offering instruction in accounting and the

213

broadcast arts. Not affiliated with any other institution.

INDUSTRIAL REVOLUTION: Universe-wide revolt, from 201 B.I. (Before Imperium) through 108 B.I., in which humans overthrew the forces of technology and industrialization.

IX-NAY: Ninth planet of Alpha-E. Neumann, known for its advanced machine culture.

J

JIM-PALMERIES: An area of mounds older than many other geographical features but still in pretty good shape.

K

KLAUSKINSKI: Skeptical as to the veracity of a religious-based rumor.

KLORMER: Comrade, buddy.

KOOLL-JUH-HERK!: "I am profoundly shocked!" Original meaning, "You all sitting there looking at me like I'm a fool."

KRAMDEN: A formal state of feud, or vendetta, between two neighboring Houses or peoples, who by mutual acknowledgment ought rightly to be pals.

KREP-LOCK: Freedmenmen low-level security device used for safeguarding chiksoop and other similar krep (see Chiksoop).

KREZNUM: Gravy.

KUMKWAT HAAGENDASZ: "The One Whose Fruit-Like Soul Is Tempered to a Soft Consistency." This is the label applied by the Boni Maroni to the X-factor, the unknown for which they were searching, the specific meaning of which none of them had the slightest idea of. Perhaps refers to a chef who is able to bring to readiness many dishes at one time; perhaps not.

L

LASERIUM AL-DILAH': "The Bright Light of the Italian Love Song." In Freedmenmen messianic legend, the redeemer from another world. See Mahdl-T.

LA-ZER-BOY BEAM: A force-field recliner capable of holding the body in a state of relaxation while providing on-demand ottoman-style foot-support.

LENNONJON: A waterproof sack used for transporting liquids.

LINK-RAY: Freedmenmen survival device consisting of an early '60's guitar player.

LITTLE STICK: (Also "Baby Stick") The secondary growth stage of the giant pretzel.

LUMPER: Freedmenmen device for summoning pretzels. Consists of a spring-packed "scoop" which compresses sugar into cubes, transmitting a signal through the ground.

LYFAH-RYLI: Fulfilled, usually with reference to an apocryphal or legendary assertion or prophecy.

MACHOOLA: Out of business; bankrupt.

MAGNETAZINE: Periodical journal, published on magnetic tape, consisting of photopix and textfax.

MAHDL-T: In Freedmenmen messianic legend, "the one who will drive us to Paradise and back."

MAHI-MAHI: The day of the arrival of the Messiah.

MAHN T'VANI: Freedmenmen food experiments, principally their attempt to create entrees via soy bean manipulation. The resulting dishes were invariably bland and without character.

MALTOSE FALCON: Bird native to Arruckus. Freedmenmen nickname: "The Sweet Bird of Youth."

MANTAN: An adviser to royalty or others in positions of power, whose function is usually to nod knowingly and, by maintaining an attitude of measured agreement, stay out of trouble.

MILANOS-2: The second planet of Milanos; known for its footwear and furniture design.

MISSIONARIA PHONIBALONICA: The arm of the Boni Maroni order charged with sowing chiliastic legends, and distributing surplus food, throughout the known universe.

MIZOUR-RI: Broad river in Freedmenmen myth.

NABE: A Freedmenmen leader. Originally, a headman of a small locale.

NOAMCHOMSKI: Neutralis Organizational Abba Mercantile Condominium Havatampa Orthonovum

Minnehaha Shostakovitch Kategorical Imperative. Huge interplanetary industrial combine managed by the Great Big Houses and the Emperor.

NOFREELUNCHES: The rigid rules of class distinction of the Imperium.

NOUVELLE ALDEBARAN: Cuisine style popular during the lifespan of Pall-Mauve'Bib, highlighted by the use of local ingredients, small portions, intense reductions, outlandish prices, and garnishes consisting of one or two unbelievably precious snow peas or baby zucchini.

NUGGET: Primary growth stage of the giant pretzel.

O

ORANGE COUNTY BIBLE: Ancient text of sacred writing, comprising the Good Old Testament, the New Improved Testament, and the Book of Regulations.

ORTHODONTOTHOPTER (Commonly, 'thopter): Winged flying vehicle consisting of a number of fixed appliances pulled by rubber bands. Expensive, but in the long run definitely worth it.

OUT-FREEKT: In Freedmenmen argot, a stranger, one from another world. So-called due to the person's usual initial response to the conditions of Arruckus.

P

PAD OF MEMOS: Freedmenmen paper tablet for jotting down little notes and things.

PAHDEDBRAH BROADCASTING SYSTEM: The official Imperial video network, known for its documentaries about exotic cultures, enlightened educational programming, and endless series of British costume dramas from Old Earth.

PEANUT BUTTER: The paste-like invention of Pall-Mauve'Bib consisting of crushed cocktail mix and nugget oil (see Cocktail Mix).

POTCHKIED (also BEER-POTCHKIED): In a state of religious intoxication; drunk.

PRETZEL: The giant snack-animal hybrid of Arruckus.

PROCTOR-SILEX: A head instructor at a Boni Maroni school.

R

RANCHO JURIS GRANDE: An investigative inquest held by the Great Big Houses.

RANKOUT: Combat via insult, invective, and insinuation.

RAZZMATAZZIA: A guerrilla raid for purposes of bedazzling and impressing the enemy.

REVVED-UP MOTHER: A holy woman. Originally, a teacher at a Boni Maroni school.

RICKENBACKER: Twelve-stringed guitar-like guitar.

RIGELIAN CLAM LEATHER: Leather fashioned from the tanned hides of Rigelian clams.

S

SALACIA SIMPLICISSIMUS: Third planet of

Beta-Fischook, and official prison planet of the Imperium.

SALTROCK: The large salt boulder that adheres to the back of the giant pretzel of Arruckus.

SCHMAI-GUNUG: The giant pretzel of Arruckus. When capitalized, refers to the pretzel-deity who rules the planet and its inhabitants. Originally translated to mean "to browse and fiddle around and window-shop enough." Also called, in adult form, the "Three-Ringed Yoke of Madness."

SCHNAGG: Made-up word meaning a blessing, a boon. Completely arbitrary.

SHANANA-: An heir designate. Lit., "The king? No, no."

SHIELD: A thin membrane of authentic animal skin surrounding the capital city of Arrucksack, used for hygienic protection while still affording maximum sensitivity.

SKROBBNIG: The withered stump of the jorj bush. Usu. used pejoratively.

STIX NIX HIX PIX: An expression of resignation, coupled with a sense of the unpredictibility of Fate, as in "What can you do?"

SUDSFEST: A Freedmenmen beer-drinking ritual, in which the men of the community sit around and drink beer.

SWEATSUIT: Clothing worn by Freedmenmen on Arruckus, the purpose of which is to promote perspiration and thus reduce bodyweight gained by the intake of beer and sugar-based desserts.

SWEAT-TENT: Freedmenmen portable shelter, made of micro-sandwich insulating material, used for maximizing perspiration of its occupants for purposes of weightloss and slimdown.

SWYSKNIFE: Weapon/appliance of the Freedmenmen of Arruckus. It consists of a number of blades, openers, and other devices collapsible into a single metal sheath. (See Church Key).

T

TALMUD TE CHING: The ancient holy text of the Jiu-Jitsu's for Jesus of the Judo-Christian Tradition.

THERMOFAX SUSPENSOR: Seating force-field in which the physical form of the sitter is copied with pretty decent accuracy.

TORAH' RA BUUM DI-'EY: Sacred scripture of the Hebrew National Salaami people.

TURBINADO: The cyclonic sugar-storm of Arruckus. All natural.

TZID: A leader, commander. Arbitrary word.

U

UPDIKE CENTAURI: A star known for its beautiful, lambent surfaces.

V

VARIETESE: Native tongue of the Freedmenmen of Arruckus. So-called because it is a variety of English, probably.

VELVEETA: "The Cheese That Cannot Die." Immortal cheese-food product from Old Earth that remains in use in the Imperium, many examples of which are still in their original cartons.

VOLKSRITR: A people or nation, particularly one with a tradition of literacy and the processing of words.

W

WALLACH-ELI: Sixth planet of Tempo Terrance, known for its cultural sophistication. Homeworld of the Boni Maroni.

WALLY: A Freedmenmen boy. Common form of address: "Gee, wally—."

WESTINGLOBE: Self-contained light source, usually frosted to provide a soft, nonglaring ambience.

Y

YOGI-BEAR: The Boni Maroni discipline of body-control. Key triggering phrase: "Yah-bahdah Bah Do."

YOGI-BERRA: The Boni Maroni discipline of mind-control. Key triggering phrase: "A thing is not over until it is over."

Z

ZIGZAGPAPER: Paper formed of pulped Tulgy wood, noted for its thin strip of adhesive gum on each sheet.

The most magnificent Science Fiction Epic Saga Series in Science Fiction Epic Saga Series History!

DOON

•

DOON MESHUGGANAH

•

MEN, WOMEN, CHILDREN, PETS OF DOON

•

LORD GOD HELP US, ANOTHER SEQUEL TO DOON

•

THE DOON REFERENCE BOOK, ATLAS, AND RHYMING DICTIONARY

•

THE DOON CATALOGUE OF QUALITY MENSWEAR FOR DAD 'N' LAD

•

The DOON boxed gift set:
The complete DOON series,
a full color poster, and a button

WHAT'S A REAL MAN'S BEST FRIEND?
A REAL DOG!

Not to mention the other hilarious titles available to you from Pocket Books.
You want fun? You got it!
Ah, what the heck. Order all of 'em.